Reader Reviews

Once I started, I read this book straight through because I was so interested to see what happened next. Rose's life with horses winds through her family involvement in her passion, from showing and breeding to the abuses of soring prevalent in the Tennessee Walking Horse training barns, tragedies and accidents, heart-warming tales and chilling lessons for any horse lover. Thank you for sharing your "horse life" with all of us, Rose.

Lori Northrup
Friends of Sound Horses Inc. (FOSH) President www.fosh.info
TWHBEA Director
Activist for saving Tennessee Walking Horses from the abuses of soring
Tennessee Walking Horse lover, breeder and rider since 1978
Parelli Level 3

As a professional full time horseman trained in the Dressage discipline, it was an interesting and educating experience to work with a Tennessee Walking Horse for the first time.

My first impression of Hallelujah was, "What a beautiful horse!" and simultaneously, "What a great attitude!" The next impression was that Rose Miller had a keen desire and interest in using classical dressage as a training method to further her stallion.

My professional training with many top Masters of the Equestrian World and graduation from the M.P.I.E.I. helped me to work with a breed of horse that moved differently from any others in the equine genre. After 35 years of professional teaching and training people and horses, working with Rose Miller and her stallion, Praise Hallelujah, is one of the highlights of my career.

Charles Sherman

I spent the next three evenings engrossed in your memoir. I found it to be quite touching. It is a very enjoyable, informative story. While I am not knowledgeable about horses, I found my reading journey into your world to be a very pleasant experience.

LaMonte Heflick
Speech, Hearing, and Language Pathologist (Roosevelt K-2 Primary)
Japanese/Chinese (Elkhart Community Schools)
Author of *Pup Fiction Books* and *The Adventures of Thin Than*
www.rempub.com

Rose Miller's *The Horse That Wouldn't Trot* is a book that I could read over and over again. She touches upon the human and equine hardships faced in her life in a heartwarming and self-effacing manner. The chapters that address the soring situation are concise without being morbid. Her artful weaving of the plight as well as the history of the showing and breeding practices of the Tennessee Walking Horse will educate as well as entertain readers.

Nya Bates
Bates Gaited Horses
www.batesgaitedhorses.com

The Horse That Wouldn't Trot offers an intriguing look at the world of horses through the eyes of a horse lover and horse owner. It is an honest, heartwarming portrayal of the highs and lows associated with the love and care of horses. It specifically guides the reader through the issues and problems facing the Tennessee Walking Horse world, which are enlightening, yet discouraging. This book is awe-inspiring and once you open it, you will be hooked! I loved this book.

Lori Snyder-Lowe
2009 NWHA President, www.nwha.com

I finished your book and I really enjoyed it. I *did* find it to be a page turner. There were times I felt I was physically there myself watching you and the horses and having a great time and then there were times I had to grab a tissue or two. It was also very informative about so many things I knew so little about.

The whole breeding process, from what goes on with the stud to the birth of the foal was enlightening. Showing the horses and the different level of shows, but most importantly the entire soring issue was revealing, interesting - and very sad! I also enjoyed reading about you and your daughters.

Your tribute to Sharon was so heartwarming. I can only imagine how proud she is of you. When I finished reading, I wished there was more - that is definitely a sign of a good story.

I am so happy you asked me to be a guinea pig! I don't find time to read many books and so often I don't finish. I had no problem finishing this one. I wish you nothing but the best of luck and hope and pray it is everything you are wishing for.

Shelia Berkey, horse owner and trail rider of gaited horses

This is a book about a horseperson who set lofty goals and put her whole self into accomplishing them. She shares this along with other events in her life in a very open manner. Her willingness to reveal her struggles and frustrations gives the reader permission to accept life's disappointments. It held my interest and kept me up past bedtime to finish a chapter, and then read another chapter or two.

Steve & Mary Jane Wirts, early (1970's) promoters and breeders of sound flat shod pleasure show and trail horses which did much to bring the pleasure Walker to its present day popularity.

Love it, love it, love it. This book will hold the interest of the horse lovers and those who know nothing about horses. It is an easy read. It is sad, funny and serious. It deals with life issues as well as animal issues.

I found myself not wanting to put it down, when I did, I could not wait to get back to the story to see what was going to happen next.

Truly a great story!

Sally Billings, owner of a rescued and un-ridable Thoroughbred race horse

Thank-you for allowing me to share in a very small way, the telling of your story. I have learned a great deal, cried, and smiled as I read. I feel I was guided to your door, and have gained confidence and encouragement from your story.

Mary Beth Kirkpatrick, new horse owner

Dedication

This book is lovingly dedicated to the memory of my daughter Sharon, who encouraged me to believe in myself, inspired the writing of *The Horse That Wouldn't Trot*, and shared my love for all animals.

Prologue

When I began writing *The Horse That Wouldn't Trot,* it was with the idea of telling heartwarming, entertaining and poignant stories of my horses. But as I wrote about my amazing horses, I soon realized there was another issue that greatly affected my life—the technique of *soring* which is used to get the Tennessee Walking Show Horses to gait in a flashy but abnormal way.

Soring was made illegal in 1970 with the Horse Protection Act, but it still exists, thwarting attempts to completely stop it. In 2006 more public awareness through articles exposing soring in horse magazines such as *Equus, The Horse and Horse Illustrated*, has brought tremendous gains to ending this abuse.

When I shared my unpublished manuscript with a new horse acquaintance and author, she was incensed, telling me I should not have supported the national breed organization, bred or showed Tennessee Walking Horses, as my doing so perpetuated the problem.

Her comments caused some soul searching. Would the Tennessee Walking Horse be better off if I had gone home after my very first show in 1979, and never returned? If I had not begun breeding these smooth-gaited riding horses would it have mattered? I came to the conclusion the answer was "no." Stepping away from the breed and the problem wouldn't make it go away. Soring is deeply entrenched. It is a way of life for those who do it.

As time has gone on, more people owning these marvelous horses have worked long and diligently against soring through many avenues. New organizations were formed for showing only sound (un-sored) horses. Breeding naturally-gaited horses for show and trail riding is a big undertaking. Exposing this abusive practice through public awareness is essential, and public outcry is indispensable.

The Horse That Wouldn't Trot is the narrative of my journey to become a true horsewoman. You will meet several stallions, mares and young horses each with extraordinary tales to tell, and while this was never meant to be about horse training, you can discover gems of wisdom that were hard earned by trial and error. First and foremost, *The Horse That Wouldn't Trot* was written for horse and animal lovers everywhere to enjoy.

Thanks for sharing my journey.

The Horse That Wouldn't Trot

A Life with Tennessee Walking Horses: Lessons Learned
and Memories Shared

By Rose Miller

First published by Dog Ear Publishing
4010 W. 86th Street, Ste H
Indianapolis, IN 46268
www.dogearpublishing.net

ISBN: 978-160844-264-5

This book is printed on acid-free paper.

Printed in the United States of America

Table of Contents

CHAPTER ONE

The Dream Begins

I sat upon my nervous stallion waiting to enter the big oval ring. It was Championship night. My horse was fidgeting and pacing the small warm-up area. Was he nervous because I was nervous? For a week I debated whether to show him at this big show—the biggest in the world for my breed. The Amateur Championship class had five judges positioned around the large show ring. There would be little room for error. And yes, I was nervous. A nervous wreck. No wonder my horse was fretful. He bobbed his head up and down as if he was saying, "Yes, yes, yes." But what he really meant was, "Let's get this show on the road or get out of here!"

I'd been showing my horses for ten years, but this was different. Now I had a trainer for my new horse I had owned only a few months, and we were playing in the big league. This event had been a goal since I was a child, but now I faced the realities of failure only an adult can appreciate. It had seemed so simple that day when I was four years old and excitedly sharing my wondrous epiphany with my parents: we should move to a farm and raise horses!

Dad knew I loved horses. On our way home from church each Sunday, we faithfully stopped by the small stable in town to pet the two black horses who lived there, but living on a horse farm was certainly not in his plans. Dad and Mom had just shaken their heads at my imagination back then, but strange things have a way of happening, and when I was eight years old, we moved to a mountaintop farm in north central Pennsylvania. Our animal menagerie consisted of several cows (including the most wonderful pet Jersey cow, Buttercup) chickens, ducks, peacocks, a lamb and eventually two horses—Smokey and Sugarfoot. We didn't raise any horses, but as far as I was concerned, my childhood with few exceptions was perfect.

When I was nineteen, I married my husband, Hal, and we moved to Elkhart, Indiana, where he began his chiropractic career. Because he'd been raised on a farm in Kansas and loved country life as much as I did, eventually we bought a small farm in the area. We enjoyed a couple of idyllic years living on our little homestead and adding a daughter and son to our family.

On Palm Sunday in 1965, one of the many deadly tornadoes that ripped Indiana and the Midwest apart demolished our little farm. Our lives were spared but our animal family was lost. What wasn't killed in the tornado strike had to be sold. The most devastating occurrence was selling Buttercup, who

Hal and I had brought to Indiana with us. With our little farm in ruins and our lives in disarray, there was no place for a cow. I was more destroyed by this incident than losing all our worldly possessions. Buttercup wasn't just a cow; she had been my best childhood friend and confidant. After this shocking experience, I wanted nothing more to do with animals. Losing them was just too horrible. We moved to a small house, then to a large, beautiful home on the river. Hal heard no more about farms and horses.

It was during our life on the Elkhart River that our ten-year-old daughter, Sharon, decided she had to have a horse. Sharon was only four years old when we lost our little farm to the tornado, and other than the dog, Lady, she didn't have access to other animals. Perhaps that "horse gene" had been passed from mother to daughter. At any rate she was adamant she needed a horse.

Six years had passed since the tornado, and horses and other animals began to pull at my heart strings again. Sharon's fulfilled desire for a horse was the beginning of the second phase of my life with horses. Most fortunate for the implementation of my future venture into the equine world was the support I was given by Hal. Although he was raised on a Kansas homestead, he wasn't imbued with an intense devotion to animal life. His dad farmed for awhile with large draft horses, but Hal didn't become a horse lover. In fact our early relationship nearly came to an abrupt halt the day he threw a clod of dirt at my much loved horse, Smokey. Hal was on vacation and digging a ditch for a water line for my parents on our Pennsylvania farm, and Smokey was in his way. "Shoo, scram you darn horse," Hal shouted as he tossed a big dirt ball in the horse's direction. I was incensed. How dare he! Happily for our future life together and my horse endeavors, Hal loved *me* and became a longsuffering mender of farm fences and horse stalls.

After Sharon's declaration that she needed a horse, we ended up with three of them on a subdivision lot where there really shouldn't have been any. A three-quarter acre lot on a river which flooded easily, in an area of many homes and a school, was not the perfect place for horses. During the hot, humid summer days, the aroma of horse wafted not so gently over the houses and I traipsed door to door apologizing, sometimes bringing home-made chocolate chip cookies to the neighbors closest to the horse smell. After two years of living as horse suburbanites, Hal and I planned a move.

We found the ideal spot in the country, close enough for Hal to commute to work, a good school for the children, nearby shopping areas, and 50 acres that we would use as a horse farm. Almost 30 years from the time I came down the stairs as a young child, proclaiming we needed a horse farm, it was actually going to happen.

While living at the River House, we acquired Apache, Sharon's first horse who was a barely-trained Appaloosa and had some roguish tendencies. One day Apache, in an ornery snit of stubbornness, lay down with Sharon on his back in a potato field and refused to get up. Sharon walked home from the neighbor's field crying, and that was when I realized I didn't know as much about horses as I thought I did. Selling Apache was out of the question because Sharon had fallen in love with him—a very common situation with girls and horses—so we kept Apache and bought Ranger, a quiet, older, very well-trained Quarter Horse.

Sharon and Apache

Ranger did an absolutely superb job teaching Sharon to ride; she became quite accomplished and was fearless. I couldn't give him a higher recommendation. He was a great babysitter horse—except for one significant phobia.

In the 1970s, traffic on our county road was not excessive, and we could ride safely several miles around the farm. As soon as Sharon got home from school, we saddled up and went riding. She rode Ranger and I rode Apache. One day we were having a marvelous late afternoon ride, talking animatedly to each other, not paying complete attention to our horses. Suddenly, Ranger took a leap sideways off the road and into a farmer's field. Sharon stayed on and somehow managed to stop Ranger who was heading for home in double time.

I sat on Apache with my heart in my mouth seeing this unfold, wondering how it would end. It was a helpless feeling to realize there really wasn't anything I could do. For once, Apache was not the troublemaker, and he was watching Ranger and Sharon himself wondering what all the fuss was about. The fuss turned out to be pigs.

The farmer had a pig pen by the road. Apparently, even before we reached it, the smell alerted Ranger that strange "attack animals" lurked ahead. We were lucky there was no fence along that side of the road, or Ranger and Sharon would certainly have become entangled with a disastrous outcome. Ranger was so spooked that he was dangerous, and I ended up leading him some distance away with Sharon riding Apache. I discovered some horses have an extreme and unreasonable fear of pigs.

After getting to our new farm, I began Apache's training in earnest and he turned out pretty darn good. He would never be my favorite horse, but we had been through a lot together and he'd been a good teacher in the school of hard knocks. Because I was planning on embarking upon an Arabian breeding project, I decided to sell Apache.

A pleasant man answered my ad and he seemed very knowledgeable, not a green or first-time buyer, and he wore cowboy boots and a cowboy hat; however, I still told him all about Apache's possible dirty tricks. One of the greatest compliments I ever got in my life as a trainer was from this gentleman after he rode Apache. He dismounted and said in a quiet voice, "I can see this horse has had some good training." I was so pleased I was beaming, but I tried to play it cool. He bought Apache and moved him a few miles away. When I traveled that country road, I would see him in his new home and pasture. He always looked good and I was content with the out-come.

Ranger also found a good new home with another beginning rider.

Sharon was enthusiastic about the budding horse-raising venture and wasn't too sorry to see Apache and Ranger leave. Soon there would be other more challenging horses for this accomplished young girl to ride.

Roger was our second child and our only son. He thought the farm was great because it had machinery. Forget the horses. Michal Elaine, our third child, also seemed rather disinterested in the horses. She had more fun tormenting her older brother Roger. Chessa, the baby of the family, enjoyed her next-door cousins and Grandma Sara. I think Hal just hoped his family, especially his wife, would live through the exciting and perhaps dangerous days that might loom ahead for us in our novice horse venture.

Horses are wonderful creatures, and although I loved them with a strong passion, I was soon to learn that loving them was not enough. A major education was about to begin...

CHAPTER TWO

Oh, My Aching Back

"Hurry up, Sharon, let's ride before it gets any later. Then we will feed the horses!" If we hurried we could ride before it got too dark to be safe.

Sharon was as gung-ho about riding as I was again becoming. Maybe more so because her back didn't hurt; she was younger and crazy about horses. My big problem was my lower back and Hal was continually treating it. Having a chiropractor for a husband was proving to be providential—and cost effective.

My first horse training project was a two-year-old registered Half-Arabian mare whom I bought with the intention of starting my breeding venture, and riding. I loved Arabian horses the best of all the breeds. They were gorgeous, elegant and flashy. When I started working with my horses those many years ago, starting a horse under saddle was called "breaking." Fortunately for me and the beautiful chestnut mare, neither of us "got broke." Years later the new type of horse training called Natural Horsemanship and horse trainers called Horse Whisperers became very popular with horse owners who had either contributed to or inherited a horse with major problems. It was a much gentler way, a way of becoming connected with one's horse, becoming partners, gaining trust, conquering bad habits and sometimes even becoming soul mates.

Such a horse was Aliraf, an older pure-blooded Arabian horse. I thought Aliraf was quite a find. He did some tricks, was trained in dressage, was very beautiful with his chiseled and refined Arabian head, and he was relatively inexpensive as his owner was moving and wanted a good home for him. When I was a child dreaming of my first horse, Aliraf was what I had envisioned, something like Walter Farley's Black Stallion. Instead, as a child I got wonderful old Smokey, a small draft-type horse. Smokey was the perfect horse for a young horsewoman but in my youthful ignorance, I had desired a splendid saddle horse.

My husband and I hadn't yet moved to our farm when I bought Aliraf and took him home to the River House. He had been there only a few days when I had my first really bad horse accident. I tied him up in the little shed Hal had built for me to groom and fuss over him. I picked up one hind foot to clean out the dirt when suddenly he whipped me to the side of the shed slamming my right shoulder into the wall with a sickening thud.

I was in such agony I could barely breathe. I crawled slowly up the flowered embankment to our patio back door and screamed for Hal. It was most fortunate that my accident happened on a weekend when Hal was home. He heard me yelling, and after a quick look, he took me to the hospital where it was determined that my shoulder had been dislocated and would require surgery.

My accident was one of those things that was a mixture of my ignorance and a horse's really, really bad habit. Aliraf was a confirmed halter-puller. I discovered I could not tie him to anything at anytime, ever. I had a hard time accepting his former owner's negligence in telling me about Aliraf's dangerous habit. I would still have purchased the horse, had I known, but I would have been more careful. In my ignorance, I hadn't asked if the horse had any bad habits, as I was too excited to find such a stunning and well-trained horse. Now I had a painful, injured shoulder in a sling. I was not happy.

After the healing time, the pin was removed from my right shoulder and my treatment began. Therapy consisted of painting the walls of our new house and many nights I went to bed in total misery. I'm not sure I would have stuck with structured therapy that caused me that much pain. I couldn't raise my arm above my head, but to paint the walls I kept pushing it to the limit. I recovered completely and a lesson with horses was learned the hard way.

Before our new house was completed, but with the barn and a pasture horse-ready, we moved the horses, our dog Lady, and my six geese to the farm in late summer of 1973—the same year the great Secretariat won the Triple Crown. Apache, Ranger and Aliraf were ridden the few miles to their new home. They were glad to have a pasture and a real barn and I set out to break Aliraf of his terrible halter-pulling habit. God apparently suffers fools because this was one horse and bad habit I had no business tackling.

When it became apparent that Aliraf would rather break his neck by thrashing back and forth and backing up until it looked like he would stop breathing and his big black Arabian eyes would pop out of his head rather than stand tied to anything, I gave it up. It was something I would just have to live with. With the later day join-up and new horsemanship techniques, I might have been able to conquer his fear of tying, but at that time I was too new at horse training. Smokey hadn't prepared me for any of this foolishness.

How horses develop the halter-pulling habit is hard to pinpoint, but it usually happens after a traumatic incident while the horse is tied. Perhaps he is spooked or scared and he reacts by forcefully backing up and hitting the end of the tied rope frightening him even more and causing him to fight. By now he has lost all reason and the only thing he can think of is getting away from the offending rope. It could take several episodes, or just one, depending upon the disposition of the horse and the degree of fright. Usually something will break, perhaps the halter, rope or what he was tied to, and he then is free. In his mind, he has figured out that if he fights hard enough and long enough, he will get himself out of what he sees as a dangerous situation.

If none of the equipment breaks, the horse can be injured badly even breaking his neck, or at the very least, pulling muscles, making him sore and uncomfortable. Some horses can be retrained with much patience and time, but it was recommended to me by trainers I consulted to just accept the fact he couldn't be tied.

One of the many concepts horse people all over the world understand is that one cannot depend on a horse never to cause harm to himself or his person. It is a horse's nature to be the prey animal, the one being eaten, and his first line of defense is to run, run, run, and fight as needed in order to run. The horse can't be blamed. It is his genetic make-up. This is the basic premise of the new horse whisperers such as Pat Parelli, John Lyons, Clinton Anderson, Monty Roberts and others. These men with their gentle methods have become bywords to the current horse-owner population. In ignorance people act like predators to their horse who is a prey animal. The goal of these new instructors is to show the horse the person can be a quiet and safe leader of their herd of two.

As my horse education grew, I learned that an older horse such as Ali-raf could be more of a problem than a young untrained one. Faema was a good example. She took to riding as though she had been born knowing how. Later when I had my young horses for sale, people who came to me started out with the sentence, "I want to buy an older horse, about ten or twelve."

"Why?" I asked.

"Well, because they have experienced life and are well trained—so they will be safe," was the answer.

Then I explained the difference between Aliraf and Faema. A young horse with a clean slate can be a better buy than an older animal with problems. But not always.

Sir Galahad entered our life in a big way. He was two years old, also a Half-Arabian, and would need training. His coat was a light strawberry color that would over time change into grey and he had a stunning black mane and tail. He was quite a looker, and quite the character. Sir simply loved life; whatever was happening, he wanted to enjoy it.

He and Sharon bonded right away. Sir was green broke, just started under saddle, much the same as Apache had been but both Sharon and I knew more about horses now and were better riders. Sir loved to gallop and Sharon loved nothing more than to let him go full out. I had enjoyed doing that with my childhood horse Smokey, but there is a big difference in the speed of a draft horse and an Arab. Smokey was more like riding a circus horse; Sir could really go. Sharon and Sir gave me the first of many gray hairs.

"Mom, want to race?" Sharon asked.

"Not on your life, not in a million years." I replied.

What was that child thinking? Our riding times together were much more sedate. Some walking and a little trotting—time to chat about school and do some mother-daughter bonding. How much better could it be done than from the back of a horse?

"Only kidding, Mom." Sharon said playfully.

Sir had one bad habit, and again it was because the horse is a prey animal. He would spook jumping sideways—or, just as bad, stop on a dime—all because he imagined something terrible was going to jump out from behind that rock, tree or a clump of grass. What made his spooks so bad was the rider didn't know when they were coming; what Sir saw with his eyes—or imagination—the rider almost never saw. He had the reputation of more rider dumps than any horse we have ever had. He never did anything out of meanness and he wasn't jumpy on the ground, just when you were riding, and he thought an ogre was about to get him.

Sir would not have been a good buy for a beginner, but he would have been a perfect horse for the new join-up type training. The idea of this training is if the horse joins to the human partner and trust is given, the horse will not need to look for those scary monsters behind every tree. The horse will feel safe because his human leader is his surrogate boss mare of the wild herd—the horse who leads them to safety.

Now that we had a real farm, I felt I was ready for my first horse-breeding experience. Breeding Faema, my young mare, to a friend's pure-bred Arabian stallion proved easy, and eleven months later in the spring, little Sahara was born. She was a chestnut filly, very tiny and truly delightful. I was fortunate the birth went well since it was the mare's first time and mine as well. The only problem was one I created for myself.

Sahara couldn't seem to find the right place to nurse and I panicked. If she didn't get that first milk with the colostrum right away as the horse books say, I was sure something dire would happen. Plus it seems Mother Nature made it most difficult for a foal to suckle. The mare's udder is rather small, nothing like a milk cow's, and tucked way up between her hind legs. A foal has to be a contortionist to bend its head up and under to grab a teat to suck.

I tried to help her nurse. Boy, was that a mistake. I was all alone; the mare was cooperative, but Sahara wanted nothing to do with being pushed into her mother's udder. I tried to get her to suck on my finger. She wouldn't. She sat on my arms as I pushed her under her mom's hind legs. Finally, I gave up in frustration and left them alone, sure I'd end up losing my first foal. The only thing I had accomplished was to sprain my own back. I went back an hour later after taking Advil and putting on some liniment, and found the filly nursing just fine. Experience has taught me that if you give them some time, they will almost always figure it out.

Experience also taught me some important lessons about my own physical abilities. The Arabian horses we owned, raised and trained all had spirited trots. The horses were smallish and their legs pounding the ground when they trotted caused jarring of the rider, namely me. Sharon never seemed to mind it one bit; in fact, like many other people, she reveled in it.

A rider can post on trotting horses by rising out of the saddle seat for every other stride of the horses' forelegs. By so doing, one can protect oneself from the bounce of the trot—up, down, up, down. That takes some skill and effort, and although it is good exercise, it is work. Some horses have very gentle trots and are easy to sit. In a show ring, the Arabian trot is beautiful to behold, very showy and exciting, but my back was starting to have trouble with the jolt it received as I rode.

My husband, the chiropractor, was doing lots of work on my back to keep me comfortable and riding. One day he came home from the office and told me that he had just heard about a horse that didn't trot. It was called a Tennessee Walking Horse. He strongly suggested that I check it out—and quickly. Bless his heart; he knew that I would rather suffer than give up riding, so he had never suggested it.

Perhaps if I had not been so in love with the Arabian horse, but had gotten into another breed that had a soft, easier trot, or if my back had not been an issue, I never would have entered my next new and very exciting endeavor. My life was about to change—big time.

CHAPTER THREE

The Tennessee Walking Horse

A Tennessee *Walking* Horse? What on earth was that? I had never heard of the breed. I was in love with the gorgeous Arabian horses that I couldn't ride any longer. What a pity. Some research was in order.

The Tennessee Walking Horse (Walking Horse or Walker) is an all-American breed. It was developed in the United States as were the Morgan Horse and the American Quarter Horse. The Walking Horse was genetically engineered by mating several different recognized breeds of trotting and pacing blood together and by a sort of accident, fate, or luck, a new breed of horse evolved—a horse that didn't trot *or* pace, but did a smooth, gliding, comfortable gait.

Many horse lovers are familiar with Figure, foaled in 1789, considered to be the foundation sire of the Morgan Horse. Marguerite Henry made this little Vermont horse well known with her book, *Justin Morgan Had a Horse.* His bloodline is one that contributed much to several breeds, including the Tennessee Walking Horse. Figure was a prepotent sire. His offspring had his characteristics; they were on the small side but had great strength and speed for a small horse and were usually bay in color. As he became known for these attributes, many mares were bred to him over the course of his 32-year life span.

The foundation sire of the Tennessee Walking Horse breed was prepotent too, but his strength was in passing on the smooth running walk that makes the Tennessee Walking Horse famous and desirable. Here is a brief history of the beginning of the Tennessee Walking Horse breed, derived from the book, *The Echoes of Hoofbeats,* by Bob Womack.

A man named George Ely purchased a chestnut stallion with white markings in Lexington, Kentucky, in the early 1880s. This horse, Elyria, was foaled in 1882; his dam was Maggie Marshall who was a Morgan Horse. Elyria was a great trotter with a record of 2:25 ¼, very fast for racing down the one-mile track with the high-wheeled sulkies of those days. Mr. Ely was so pleased with Elyria that in 1886 or 1887, he returned to Lexington and purchased Maggie Marshall and her new little black stallion colt. When the colt matured, Mr. Ely began training him, but Allan, as he was named, refused to trot—very much disappointing Mr. Ely.

Allan was put to stud, but many said he was too small for a breeding stallion, and the mares brought to him were not of the quality to produce good colts, so about seven years later the horse was started on a series of downward sales. Over the years Allan was traded many, many times always depreciating in value. Eventually, however, something would happen that changed horse history.

When the first Tennessee settlers came over the mountains from Virginia and the Carolinas, some were riding on horses with easy gaits. These horses undoubtedly contained the blood of the Narragansett Pacers from which the early gaited stock in the colonies was produced. Late in the eighteenth and early in the nineteenth centuries, the area nurtured a specific breed known as the Thoroughbred racing horse which was one of the first to add refinement to this new easy-gaited breed that was developing.

This combination would produce some top-notch gaited riding horses, but it was noted that horses from these unions that had as much as fifty percent running and consequently trotting blood, were difficult to "gait." This was the problem that the new breeders of gaited horses in Tennessee were having. It wasn't always possible to get a foal that would do the smooth gait they desired. It would be old black Allan who one day would make the difference.

In 1903 Allan, the little black stallion, was offered to Mr. James R. Brantley along with a fine jack (a male donkey). Mr. Brantley wanted the jack, but didn't know about Allan. Having heard about Allan's exceptional pedigree, he checked it out, riding almost a hundred miles to investigate. He discovered the original registration in the *American Trotting Registry* and saw for himself that the claims were true. In addition there was a notation stating that Onward, Allan's grandsire, was the greatest stallion living or dead. He hitched his favorite mare Gertrude to the buggy, and went to make the purchase.

Allan was a gentle, dependable horse. Brantley's son rode the little stallion to school and left him tied to a tree during school hours. Allan's chief gait under saddle was a running walk which he performed comfortably and smoothly. Mr. Brantley liked old Allan and the saddle horses he produced so he bred his much-loved buggy mare, Gertrude, to him.

In 1909, Mr. Albert Dement bought Allan from Mr. Brantley with the guarantee that the little stallion would live through the breeding season. The 1910 breeding season was to be the last for Allan. On September 16, 1910, at the age of 24, the little horse that had started out as a failure, died. It is to the credit of the horsemen in the Middle Tennessee area that the blood of Allan was allowed to mix with the good, gaited stock of that area to perpetuate the "Allan" strain of horses.

Albert Dement was more than a horse breeder. He had a vision of what a good smooth riding saddle horse should look like and how it should move. One of his main goals was to establish a breed of horse that would *consistently* produce gaited offspring. It would be old Allan who provided the genetics to produce this consistency. (Actually many other notable stallions of that day produced gaited stock, but following his death, Allan was renamed Allen F-1 and was accepted as the Foundation Sire of the Tennessee Walking Horse.)

Throughout more than a century of meticulous breeding, the Walking Horse had come to possess some of the endurance of the Thoroughbred, the substance and weight of the Standardbred, the smooth lines and docility of the Morgan, the style and quality of the American Saddle Horse, all the while giving the rider the smooth gait for which they have become famous.

On April 27, 1935, the Tennessee Walking Horse Breeders' Association of America (TWHBEA) was formed, and the Tennessee Walking Horse became an official breed, a real American!

The gait of the Tennessee Walking Horse is a true walk, just like every horse does, but it is done faster for the "flat walk" and even faster for the "running walk." In performing these walks, at no time do the horse's feet all leave the ground at one time as happens when a horse trots. For this reason, there is no jarring motion. Because this gait is a speedy walk, the horse's head bobs or nods as he goes along. "If he isn't nodding, he isn't walking," is a true fact, often spoken by experienced Walking Horse folk. A rider seen on a good Walker seems not to move, the rider's head moves along in a steady line, while the horse's head nods up and down.

Umm…a horse that didn't trot, but had a smooth gait instead, sounded like the ticket for me and my cranky back. There was a Walking Horse breeder who also trained horses in my area; in fact he was a patient of Hal's—the one who told him about the "horse that didn't trot." I made a visit to the breeder's barn and rode one of these phenomenal horses. The motto for the breed is, *"Ride one today, buy one tomorrow,"* and that is just what we did. This trainer knew of an older, gentle mare, and Hal and I made arrangements to purchase her. Her name was Missy.

CHAPTER FOUR

The Glide Ride Begins

Old Missy had only one eye, but otherwise she was rather pretty. She was a strawberry roan, having chestnut hair mixed with white, and she had a light blond mane and tail. She had lost her left eye as a young horse, so over time she'd adjusted to being partly blind. She was very dependable, calm, and she had a smooth gait. I bred her to the trainer's stallion, and I was now in the Tennessee Walking Horse breeding business.

I loved riding Missy, but Sharon still loved riding Sir Galahad, our Arabian horse. We soon discovered an age-old problem of riding trotting and Walking Horses together. The Walkers could out-walk a trotter when the trotter walked, but the trotter could trot faster than the Walker could gait. We just couldn't seem to get together; one or the other was always ahead. If the rider tries to push the Walking Horse past the comfort zone of his gait, the horse usually will break or mess it up somehow, starting to pace or trot himself. Although a well-bred Walking Horse is born with the genetic structure of the gait bred in him, it may take some training to get him to gait consistently under saddle. Bad riding, like pushing it to keep up with a trotting horse, can ruin a gaited horse. All these things and more I would find out for myself as I continued along the path with this marvelous breed.

Hal rode Missy one time that I remember. His idea of riding was a little different from mine. I loved to gait along on the trimmed paths, enjoying the glide ride with no discomfort, coming back to the barn after a smooth ride with a big smile of contentment on my face. Hal, on the other hand, took Missy on a field trip into our woods through brush and who knows what else. He was exploring—a guy thing, I guess. Somewhere along the way he dismounted and tied her to a tree. After awhile, Missy came back to the barn leaving Hal in the woods. Apparently that was not her idea of riding either.

Missy was a favorite of my children and nieces who learned to ride on her. Her gait was not show perfect, but it was smooth and she cantered nicely. She had several babies for us and we kept her for quite some time. I heard of another Walking Horse mare in the country close by and went to check her out. Mandy seemed pleasant. I rode her extensively at her home farm and then bought her. I thought she would be a suitable horse for Hal as she was so quiet. At this point in our horse farm life, I was determined to get a very busy Hal involved with riding.

Later in the evening after she was delivered to the farm, I saddled her for my husband and was ready for him to be pleased with his new horse. Things did not work out quite that way. Mandy seemed to have undergone a complete personality change since I rode her at her old home. She was, in a word, nuts. Hal mounted and she zoomed around the pasture like a mad hornet. She wasn't dangerous as in bucking, spooking or totally running away; she just acted as if she had a bee on her rump.

Hal dismounted, handed me the reins and walked to the house. I don't recall his exact words, but he definitely was not overjoyed with his new horse. As I remember it, that may have been the last time he rode. From then on he was content to hear about the horses, fix the things they were continually breaking and pay the feed bills. This set the pattern for the rest of the New Acre horse farm venture. I was left to my own devices.

Fortunately for me and my horse undertaking, the girls, Sharon, Michal and young Chessa, loved the horses. Son Roger not so much. I tried to get him involved, but picked the wrong horse for his first ride. Sir thought Roger would love a fast gallop around the small paddock. Roger did not. I became much better at teaching people to ride and picking the proper horses as time went on.

I didn't enjoy riding Mandy either. The children and I rode the county road square mile, four miles around, and back home. How she knew when we had gone half way and were heading home, I don't know. We didn't stop and turn around, but somehow she always knew. And at that exact point, it became a challenge to get home at anything less than full-out speed. It was suggested to me that she had possibly been tranquilized before I rode and bought her. I will never know, but she was certainly a different horse when she got to my farm.

It was quite apparent that Mandy was not going to work out, but what to do with her—she would be a hard sell. She had developed the bad habit called barn sourness: she wanted to come back home. Some horses won't leave the barn or they keep trying to turn around and go back. Mandy wasn't that bad, but still she was not enjoyable. I didn't have the knowledge or patience to retrain her. Plus Mandy had an unexplainable gait. I studied it many times and could never really figure out what she was doing with her feet, but it was fast and smooth. Someone had likely enjoyed her fast speed and had never taught her to slow down and actually walk; she was always ridden at speed—another way to ruin a good horse. When I began training horses, I always made sure they knew how to walk slowly.

The trainer who sold Missy to me took Mandy in on a trade and I got another Walker, one he had raised. Her name was Shadow's Angel and she was a big mare, bigger than anything I had ridden since Smokey, my childhood draft horse. She was to that date the best quality Tennessee Walking

Horse I had owned. Angel was a red roan with white hairs mixed with brownish red and had a darker brown mane and tail. She had two white stockings on her hind legs which made her look fancy. Her face was emblazoned with a wide, white stripe that nearly encompassed her eyes. She was young, sweet and gentle, and could be bred and shown if I ever wanted to get into showing. Because I was now a breeder of Walkers, I promptly bred her to the trainer's stallion and got a pretty brown filly named Sassafras, or Sassy.

I began my Tennessee Walking Horse adventure in 1975 after breeding, training and riding the Arabians for two years. The Walking Horses were the horses of my future and soon I sold all the Arabians except Sir who was Sharon's favorite horse. I donated Aliraf to Loveway, a local riding program for physically and mentally handicapped adults and children. Loveway was among the first of its kind in the nation and is still going strong today. Many of the horses they use are donated for one reason or another. Aliraf was gentle and did well with children, but his handler couldn't tie him to anything. The old Arabian got used to wheelchairs and the loading ramp used for the children to mount their horses, and was there until he passed away.

Our Walking Horse herd kept expanding and in short order I had several mares to breed and I bred them all to my new friend's stallion. As I raised and trained these Walking Horses, I came to realize the area around us was building up fast. In only four years, it was becoming more difficult, and sometimes even dangerous, to enjoy a pleasurable ride along the county roads. There was more traffic, many large trucks and other horse-frightening vehicles. Riding a horse along the side of the road when one came up behind us or zoomed past us from the front was becoming hazardous. There also was the strong possibility of hurting your horse's feet or legs on debris hidden in the grass.

One beautiful fall day it had happened to me. My horse stepped on a broken pop bottle and cut the back of his ankle. I could easily have been injured myself as the horse reacted to the injury. I walked home leading my limping and bleeding horse, and told myself I was the mother of four children, had a doting husband who expected me to return home in one piece, and I could not afford to be hurt by something that was preventable. I needed to find another way to enjoy my horses.

The local gentleman who sold me my first Walking Horses and bred my mares was also a trainer and showed horses for his clients. I remember one day standing on the corner of a street in downtown Elkhart, watching his truck and trailer leaving for a horse show and thinking wistfully that I wished that could be me. I finally got brave enough to start the ball rolling for my first show. Angel was a good horse; her gaits were not exceptional, but they were adequate.

In the summer of 1979, Sharon, Michal, two nieces and I went to our first show in Auburn, Indiana, with Angel who was pregnant. The show was a small one, and we really didn't know what we were doing, but how hard is it to enter a ring and go around and around until the judge tells you to turn around, go in the other direction and finally to come into the center and stand? I wore a borrowed riding suit, used my regular everyday saddle, no fancy stuff. I wasn't sure I would like showing horses and was smart enough not to spend a lot of money until I was certain.

We only competed in one class, but we got a third place ribbon out of seven horses. It was not a great placing, but I was hooked! If I had gotten last place, or no place at all, my outlook and future might have been very different. We came home elated, looked at the rest of the horses and came up with a couple more that we could show.

Horse shows were usually held on a Friday and Saturday. This in itself would preclude Hal from joining us. He had a one-doctor practice and took his work seriously. I also was sure he would be bored with horse shows. He might enjoy seeing the girls and me display our horses, but there was too much time between classes. Put bluntly, my dear husband was a workaholic. Our budding show career would encompass daughters and nieces but no son or husband.

Sharon was in nursing school by this time, and she didn't have the opportunity to really get into the show spirit in a big way, but she came to a few shows and being a natural horsewoman, she and her horse always excelled. Michal, our third child, came to me one day asking if she could ride the horses with me. Up until then no one except Sharon and I had really devoted much time to riding. Roger was into tractors, cows and flying model airplanes.

Michal was about twelve when she talked to me about riding. I was surprised and so pleased to have a riding buddy again. She had really never given much attention to the horses, and I never guessed she would have the interest. I remember asking her why she decided to start riding, and I will always cherish her answer. It was short and simple. She said, "Because you do."

It was the beginning of a wonderful 19 years of riding and showing together, through her graduating from high school, graduating from Indiana State University with her degree in criminology, getting a job on the Elkhart Police Department and getting married.

Chessa, the youngest, was seven when her show career began. She grew to be the beauty of the family and with her long legs, looked the best of all of us riding a horse. Later she confided to me that she really didn't enjoy showing. She liked to ride, but not compete. What a waste of long legs, I lamented. I think she saved her competitive spirit and long legs to participate in Elkhart County's Junior Miss contest where she could sing and dance.

Sharon started her career in the medical profession, got married and eventually moved to the west side of Chicago and more or less left the horses behind. She enjoyed visiting and riding, but the drive to be a horse-woman was greatly lessened. Michal, whom I saw as an unlikely candidate at the beginning, became a wonderful horsewoman.

As the girls and I catapulted into show careers, I began to realize not all my Tennessee Walking Horses gaited the same way. Some were smooth, while others were bouncy and uncomfortable. Not only would this make a difference in horses I could exhibit in a show ring, but also, who wanted to ride an uncomfortable horse? The walking gait in the Tennessee Walking Horse is inherent. It is genetic. It is in the foals when they are born, but like the breeders of the first easy-gaited horses, getting them to breed true was a problem.

In the 1940s, as showing the Walking Horse became more popular, having a fancier horse with more action and a faster speed at the gaits became in demand. The utility Tennessee Walker who had been bred for its wonderful riding gait, and had been used to even pull a plow and wagon, was going to have another transformation, one that even today is questioned by many people. This transformation would be years in the making, but it would have a decided impact upon this breed and would cause genetic problems with the gaits of my own young horses.

CHAPTER FIVE

The Problem

It would be several years before I discovered why my young stock didn't always gait correctly, and it was time spent in frustration, anger and financial loss. People wouldn't pay as much for a pacy or trotty Walking Horse. They wanted the gliding smooth ride. I would need to go back to square one in picking breeding stock. While reading Bob Womack's book, *The Echoes of Hoofbeats*, I could see what happened to the Tennessee Walking Horse's development. It came about because of horse shows.

The early breeders of the Tennessee Walking Horse would likely turn over in their graves if they knew what changes happened to the horse they helped develop. Their utility animal became a highly-competitive animal in the show ring, and even the color preferences changed. After the popularity of the famous Midnight Sun and Merry Go Boy, black would become the favorite color and speed would be added to the gaits. To understand what happened to the Tennessee Walking Horse, one must understand the changes that occurred to the shows. A horse doing a correct walking gait was no longer considered exciting enough to draw the crowds away from the fancier Saddlebred Horses showing at the same time at some of the same local shows. People wanted excitement and that meant more speed and fancy stepping.

By 1920, the Tennessee Walking Horse was easily distinguishable from other breeds. It didn't trot, but did a gliding, overstepping smooth gait. Horse shows became more and more popular. In 1930, the first Tennessee Walking Horse Celebration Horse Show was held in Shelbyville, Tennessee, where it still is to this day. Showing a horse became a reason for owning a Tennessee Walking Horse. No longer was he just a pleasure mount to be enjoyed as a riding horse.

Judges in the late forties and early fifties found themselves with a problem. Many knew that speed and flashy steps were not the true gait of the horse, but the crowds loved it. They yelled and whooped as the horses went faster and lifted their front feet higher off the ground. The old plantation horse was not trained; he was *bred* to be what was required. Now with the coming of new times, a new type of horse was desired.

The show-horse breeders, owners and trainers wanted a different type of horse than I wanted. I desired a horse with a smooth, easy-riding gait; one with no trot, pace or bounce. The new fangled breeding was wreaking havoc with the natural riding Walker and I was paying the price. It probably didn't help my cause that my first breedings were to a show stallion. His offspring wanted to pace rather than "do the walk." Frustrated, I contemplated changing breeds again.

Another issue surfaced with the development of this new breed of Walking Horse. Because he was bred to be pacier, the trainers had to come up with a way to make the horses do the gait again. They came up with special shoes called pads or stacks, placing chains around the ankles and later, "soring" the horses by applying a caustic substance around his front pasterns (ankles). Now when the chains hit the sored pasterns, it caused a degree of pain and the horse snatched his front feet off the ground quickly, giving an exaggerated lifting of the front feet and a bigger show walk. The name given to this show type of Tennessee Walking Horse was "big lick."

Until 1990, the issue of soring the Tennessee Walking Horse wouldn't affect me and my show horses greatly. For roughly ten years I showed my pleasure horses in places and with people where this method of training was not much in evidence. I vaguely knew it existed, but I had little in common with the big lick horses or their owners. Because what I saw didn't concern me directly, and I didn't understand the enormity of the soring issue, I ignored it. Later when I purchased an awesomely-talented stallion to show in the pleasure division, this matter of soring would affect me immensely and change the way I saw things in the Walking Horse world of horse exhibition. My current problem of breeding Tennessee Walking Horses that did a natural walk was directly linked to the soring issue and I was stymied. But more on the soring of the Tennessee Walking Horse later...

CHAPTER SIX

A New Start

I was so depressed with my Tennessee Walking Horse venture and my pacing young stock, I almost gave it up. It is easy to breed horses that trot. Breeding Arabians was a breeze—raise them, break them, and ride them—except *I* couldn't ride them because their spirited trots were too hard on my bad lower back. By happenstance, I went with my husband to Michigan on a chiropractic seminar trip and met a lady who would change my life.

Carol was participating in a horse show in the same town. She was about my age, blonde, with blue eyes that sparkled when she talked about horses. Hal and I had decided he would drop me off at the show and then go on to the seminar. I desperately needed to meet and talk with other Walking Horse owners before I gave up on my gaited horse venture. I loved hearing Carol talk about the old time Tennessee Walking Horses. She had been going to the Celebration in Tennessee for years and had seen many of them in the show ring.

After some lengthy and serious discussions about the gaits of the horses, she offered the services of her stallion. Her stallion had more of the old-time bloodlines and I decided to breed two of my mares, Ebony and old Missy, to him. After I brought the mares home which were then pregnant, she told me she had just found a stallion, Delight's Headman, sired by the famous Sun's Delight, she thought I should buy. Now this was a stretch. I had never, never, I repeat, *never*, thought of owning a stallion. Having foals was one thing; dealing with a stallion was out of my league.

But Carol was a good salesperson. She persuaded me that if she could breed mares to her own stallion, so could I. She extolled this stallion's old-time blood. She reminded me this was royalty in the horse world. Sun's Delight was a very famous son of Midnight Sun, winning the Celebration World Grand Championship in 1963. He was a stunning chestnut with an attractive, refined head and sharp, pretty ears. He was line bred Wilson's Allen, meaning Wilson's Allen appeared on the pedigree of both his sire and dam. The foundation horses Hunter's Allen appeared three times, Roan Allen once, and the incomparable mare Merry Legs twice. (These were famous horses sired by old Allen F-1.)

Sun's Delight had the old-time blood that *walked*. He was not a very large horse, but he could truly perform the running walk. Even though he'd been shown at the time of soring and chains, he had a lot of natural ability and managed to survive the training techniques and still become a World Grand Champion. Sun's Delight on a horse's pedigree was a coveted thing. A son of Sun's Delight could be a great breeding stallion for the farm.

The very idea was mind-boggling to say the least. Yet an odd occurrence merely a couple years earlier came to mind and brought with it a little shiver, as if some bit of fate had already been working this horse into my life. Back in 1976, three years after Hal and I moved to our new farm and purchased our first Tennessee Walking Horses, he needed to make a trip to Georgia for another continuing-education seminar. I went along and we passed through Shelbyville, Tennessee, which hosts the Celebration each year.

Just outside of the town was a picture-perfect horse farm surrounded by pristine white fencing. In this green pasture were many mares with foals. It was Shadow Valley Farm, which would later become Sand Creek Farm. We had no idea what was there, but we couldn't help stopping to visit. We found it was a Tennessee Walking Horse stud barn. Sun's Delight was in residence along with one of his famous sons, Delight Bummin Around, himself a Celebration World Grand Champion. I had my picture taken with both these stallions, never dreaming in a million years that only a couple years later I would own a son of Sun's Delight.

Carol was positive Delight's Headman would get my breeding program going in the right direction. This grand plan would have me breeding my own mares and hopefully other outside mares for a fee. My idea all along was to make money with the horses. Having a breeding stallion and bringing in breeding fees sounded like a viable plan. It was a leap of faith, but I did it. In 1979, Carol delivered Delight to my barn and I was in

Rose and Sun's Delight

business. Delight was relatively gentle, but still a stallion with all those hormones. He was kept separated from the other horses, however my farm layout didn't allow for him to be entirely secluded, which was probably a good thing. Stallions who never see another horse except to breed can be a little too excited when they do see another one. He adjusted well and after Ebony and Misty foaled from Carol's stallion, I rebred them to Delight. That statement makes what happened sound so easy. In truth, it definitely was not.

Fortunately, I was smart enough not to try breeding a mare by myself, but it still was a near disaster. Since I had sort of fallen into having a stallion, I hadn't done any research on how to keep them, breed them, or handle them in general. I did later and had some really great laughs how in my sublime ignorance, I had done things and still survived. I didn't have the proper breeding setup which would help protect mare, stallion and handler. We just did it "behind the barn." I held the mare who had seemed receptive to Delight's advances when she was in the barn with a stall partition dividing them. A gentleman friend led Delight out of the barn. Those first steps out the door gave us advance notice that this was not going to be a friendly or long courtship. To my knowledge Delight had never bred a mare before,

but he was seven years old, so I figured surely he knew what to do with his equipment—and *did* he!

He saw the mare standing still, and I swear, never saw me at all. He paid no heed to the man holding him on the end of the rope either, but dragged him along as he dashed up to the rear of the mare, which happened to be pointed in his direction. The mare was Missy and had been mated before, but having a stallion speeding toward her like a comet was too much for her. As Delight raised himself onto his hind legs and started to throw his front ones—in the wrong direction over the *side* of the mare, she threw up her head, let out a squeal of terror and decided to leave. She bumped into my shoulder knocking me off balance and took off toward the adjoining pasture. When she got a safe distance away, we both turned to look at Delight who was having a stallion fit.

My gentleman friend was a hefty guy and he was a horseman, but Delight took us all by surprise. When Missy squealed and took off for another part of the farm, Delight snorted and reared, waving his front legs in the air. Somehow my friend held on to the angry, frustrated and screaming stallion who began running around in circles. I stayed in the field until Delight was convinced to go back into his stall.

How no one got hurt is still a mystery to me. We put the pair away for the day to let everyone cool down and tried it again the next day. This time we were more prepared for Delight's headlong dash to the mare and slowed him down to a walk. When he got to the mare, he took no time for the niceties of conversation and did the deed quickly. .

Delight would always be hard to breed. A friend reminded me, I had called that stallion a rapist. I think if a tractor had been standing in his breeding spot, he would have tried to figure out a way to breed it. There is a horse saying that a person could breed his stallion with a shoestring, meaning he was so under control that really nothing was required to direct him. For Delight even a steel cable would have been at peril of stretching.

We got a lot smarter on how to mate him to mares. It was obvious that anyone holding the mare while he serviced her was asking for trouble. Hal built an extension to the corner of the barn that looked like a solid, board fence five feet high and six feet long. Delight was then led out the front of the barn and up to the barrier. Getting him there at some semblance of a walk was always challenging. The mare was led out the back door and tied behind the barrier. Delight could hurry up to the barrier but that stopped him from racing to the mare. He was supposed to talk to her over the fence for at least a few moments before he went around it to do his job. It was much safer for all of us and even though his pillow talks weren't long, at least this system somewhat prepared the mare for his extreme sexual ardor. It was a shame I didn't then know about Pat Parelli and other horse whisper-type trainers.

That was one side of Delight. The other was the absolutely wonderful riding horse he made for Sharon. We finally sold Sir, her Arabian horse, and she and Delight bonded in the same manner and probably for the same reason—they were both full of spirit. He was too much horse for me to enjoy riding, so I happily left that up to Sharon. Another friend reminded me of the day she saw them going down our county road lickity split at a fancy running walk, feet flying, mane and tail waving and the biggest grin on Sharon's face.

He sired a lovely mare out of my good horse Angel, whose name was Sunfire by Delight. She was one of the lucky horses of the world, being bought by a lovely couple who lived in our area. They still have her even though they don't ride her anymore; she will live out her days with loving care. The colt out of old Missy was Delight's Silverheels, who had a couple owners, but received good care all his life. Both these horses were my joy; they walked from their very first steps under saddle. All I had to do was train them to stop, turn and gradually go faster keeping their walking gait. As newly born foals, they did the running walk, bobbing their little heads and striding along with the rear legs. These horses were the proof I could breed true Walking Horses with the right breeding stock.

In horseman lore there are past and present rumors that Sun's Delight was not really sired by Midnight Sun. I suppose we will never know. Before 1990 and the implementation of blood typing and DNA testing, Tennessee Walking Horses had some interesting registration issues. The registration papers didn't always go with a particular horse. I remember buying Walking Horses in the 80s and hearing tales of horses and papers not being correct.

From whatever genetic line Sun's Delight evolved, he proved himself as a great sire. Dr. Dave Whitaker, Director of the Horse Program at Middle Tennessee State University in Murfreesboro, Tennessee, is a student of Walking Horse genetic history. The college used a stallion, Hey Dare by Delight's Daredevil sired by Sun's Delight, extensively. In Dr. Whitaker's opinion, the Sun's Delight blood produced some of the most naturally-gaited Walking Horses ever bred. Dr. Whitaker told me he thought it was disappointing for the future Walking Horse gene pool that Sun's Delight stallion offspring had not been held in higher esteem. His mares were given a lot of value, but not the stallions. Because a mare can only produce one foal a year (without embryo transplants) but a stallion can produce possibly hundreds, this oversight was a great loss that would be recognized only in the later years.

Dr. James Johnson, former owner of Sun's Delight and a noted veterinarian of the day, summed up the stallion's breeding ability best when he said, "Sun's Delight is a horse of great beauty and character and we believe him to be a 'genetic freak.' He is also a pre-potent horse who has the ability to pass on those traits." Sun's Delight died on January 29, 1981, at the age of twenty-two, the same year I purchased Delight's Headman.

Sun's Delight's inherent ability would be proven in my case. I was thrilled with my Delight's offspring, but I had no idea what I had in my barn. It was too soon in my breeding career to recognize my stallion's genetic value and because he was difficult to breed, I sold him six years later to a gentleman in Idaho. Delight passed away in 1998, siring twenty-two foals in his breeding career.

Nearly twenty years later I again would be given the chance to recognize the greatness of this prized bloodline through the Pride's Gold Coin linage—in a stallion I named Praise Hallelujah who was the spitting image of Delight's Headman. Gold Coin was out of a Sun's Delight mare and in my opinion was one of the most noteworthy sires of our lifetime.

CHAPTER SEVEN

Miss Indiana

Delight sired some exceptional foals and we started showing them in the Michigan Futurity which is a class only for pre-entered horses. A fee is charged for the sire, dam and the foal. Sometimes the foal is entered before it is even born. This makes it a gamble whether the foal will be something worth showing or not. The monies from all the different participating stallion owners are jackpotted and divided. These classes paid more money to the winners, and it was a great way to get your stallion noticed.

The spring following my purchase of Delight, Carol talked me into buying a mare sired by a World Grand Champion and her nursing filly-foal sired by Pride of Midnight. Pride was a renowned stallion who over the years would make Harlinsdale Farm and himself famous by siring many, many great horses. So between the mare's own strong background and the Pride blood she'd been bred too, both mare and foal looked promising to me.

Carol and I traveled to Tennessee from northern Indiana to pick up Misty and her baby. We tied the mare in the horse trailer, but left the filly loose to lie down and to nurse as she desired. Mares generally are very careful where they put their feet and won't step on their babies, but this was a traveling trailer with stops, turns and starts. Several times we stopped and I looked in on the pair. More times than not, the foal was lying down directly under her mother's belly which made me a nervous wreck.

I named the filly Pride's Miss Indiana and that fall at the Michigan Futurity, she won the weanling, or baby class. My first futurity win! At this point in my horse career, it was the highest honor I'd received. I was nearly beside myself with pride and pleasure. Riding home in the pickup truck, I couldn't stop smiling. At last my horses were making a name for themselves and me. It was not a horse I had actually bred, but I owned it and had the sense to buy it. It was a great start with this beautiful filly. However, plans, hopes and dreams don't always work out and this was one of those times. I could never get Misty back in foal, this time to my stallion, Delight. With a limited budget and space, I could only keep horses that both showed well and were good breeding stock. Misty showed well, but that was only half of what I needed.

After trying for a couple of years to get her pregnant, I sold her to some people just to ride and show. They had a stallion of their own and kept trying to get her in foal. With veterinarian help and the use of hormones, they eventually succeeded. Unfortunately she delivered a foal who didn't live. It was sad and such a waste of great genes.

When I started Miss Indiana under saddle, it was a ride of pure pleasure. She had the very best walk of any horse I'd ever trained. I was still a novice at training for gait, so they had better have a good natural one or I was in trouble. I've since learned a whole lot about gaiting horses, but she was easy. After riding her for a few months she developed lameness in a hind leg. It was not so bad that she seemed in pain, nor did it ruin her gait, but she would never be able to show with that unsoundness. One hind leg moved farther under her body than the other, making an uneven rear stride.

A horse's stifle joint is comparable to a human knee, but it's high on his leg where leg and body meet. This joint, muscle and ligament attachment can get sprained and sore. Since those disappointing days, I have had several Walkers develop a hitch as we call it. Most of the time they can be restored to complete soundness, but I didn't know it back then and I sold her. In retrospect, that was a terrible decision. This young mare, directly by Pride of Midnight, should never have been sold even if I couldn't ride her ten feet. She would have been the best broodmare I ever owned.

Miss Indiana had a good life with a couple in Michigan who bred her to my stallion Delight and produced show winners. In my ignorance I didn't realize what I had lost until it was too late. My plans to be successful were fading with each mistake.

CHAPTER EIGHT

Horse Deals

Horse people talk about horse deals gone bad and how they were cheated by a dealer or another horse person. The time I traded Angel for Invasion's Lady, aka Frosty, was one of those, except I did it to myself. Joan lived in Wisconsin and we competed with her in the show ring. She had a rather rare white Tennessee Walking Horse mare who always seemed to win, beating us every time we were in the same class. Joan even jumped Frosty which was unusual for a Walking Horse. Frosty had some age on her, but she was a winner and I wanted more winners. Angel was a lovely horse, but she was not a winner. She placed well but not well enough for me.

I contacted Joan and asked about buying Frosty. She didn't really want to sell her, but I kept sweetening the pot. She knew Angel from the shows and finally I ended up trading Angel plus a substantial sum of money for Frosty. I always thought Frosty seemed a little thin, not bad, but some plumping up would make her more attractive; so I proceeded to give her more grain and she had lots of grass. She really enjoyed putting on those extra pounds.

I had ridden Frosty at Joan's place and we got along fine for that first short ride at the mare's home farm. But I didn't realize how much of a challenge Frosty truly was to ride. She was trained and did her gait, but she was way too speedy at everything. She went with smoke coming out her ears and fire from her nostrils. Her flat walk which was supposed to be slow and purposeful, was more like a very fast running walk, but her running walk was nearly dangerous. I actually found myself being afraid to ride her. Her canter was like riding a Kentucky Derby hopeful. There was a reason for this. As I got more educated in horses, I discovered that speed and action

trained horses seldom settle down and give a slow pleasurable ride. Joan had competed Frosty in barrel racing, pole bending and jumping. All these events required speed, and Frosty was more than willing even when I was not. I found myself hanging on for dear life, looking like a total greenhorn, as Frosty all too eagerly went through her gaits.

Joan and Frosty got along splendidly, which made riding the horse look easy. Joan knew her horse and was a great rider. I was not ready for a horse like Frosty. I called Joan once asking for advice, but Joan had little to offer. For one thing she didn't know how much I had been overfeeding Frosty, and it is hard to offer advice several states away in Wisconsin. I never got Frosty to a show, but I exhibited her once in one of the local parades. We just walked quietly among other horses. She seemed to enjoy it, as did I.

The rest of our time together was a failure. I simply couldn't get along with the hyper, white mare. Finally I called Joan and told her I was going to sell Frosty, and if she wanted her she could have her back—really cheap. Joan had owned Frosty for many years and didn't want anything bad to happen to her. This was a definite possibility with my selling her at bottom dollar and her hell-bent-for-leather approach to being ridden.

Joan agreed to take her back. When she arrived at the farm with her horse trailer and saw Frosty, she had one comment: "Oh my, is she *fat*. We will have to fix that!" I was in fact embarrassed to admit I couldn't get along with Frosty. It was quite humbling to say nothing about losing Angel who was a good, quiet mare, and money to boot. I learned a variety of things from that one experience: not every horse is right for every rider; and a horse can be a winner under the right rider and seem like an idiot under a wrong one.

Fat Frosty at the parade

Perhaps I should have asked for more help from Joan or an instructor before throwing in the towel on the mare. I was too green a rider for Frosty's spirited ways. I know I shouldn't have gotten her fat with more grain which only made her predisposition to be excitable even worse. I simply didn't have enough horse education to know she was not the horse for me. Joan had already resold gentle Angel to some people for their young child.

CHAPTER NINE

The Little Black Stallion

Always on the lookout for good breeding stock to further my hope of raising top- notch Walking Horses, I discovered a mare that was available from the owners of World Grand Champion, Threat's Supreme, who was in turn sired by World Grand Champion, Triple Threat. The mare, Ike's Big Bertha, was in foal to Threat's Supreme and I decided to purchase her. She was cheap and the reason was forthcoming. Deciding to buy was the easy part; getting her home would perhaps present more of a challenge.

Bertha had been a big lick Walker, shown with pads and chains with the customary soring practices. Somewhere along the line, she had gotten her fill of showing, trailering and soring. To show her ire to her owners and trainer, she began to continuously and viciously kick the horse trailer while she was in it. One time she managed to actually kick her hind feet out over the back of the trailer and was hung up with her hind legs off the ground and out the trailer, causing people to work frantically rescuing her before she caused herself damage. That was the day they decided to retire Bertha and breed her.

Being a broodmare would be to her liking as she wouldn't have to travel anymore. Since they owned World Grand Champion Threat's Supreme, she wouldn't have to go somewhere to be mated. That was a good plan until they decided to sell her. Other potential buyers weren't as optimistic or possibly, ignorant, about the potential problems of transporting Big Bertha as I was. I finally found a really good horse friend who was willing to make the trip for me. Bill had an idea. Many horses will travel loose in a more open-type trailer called a stock trailer. These trailers allow horses or other animals to ride untied and move around as they wish.

Miraculously this worked with Bertha. She loaded into the trailer, turned around and rode backwards the whole way to our farm. I never had occasion to haul her again until I sold her many years later, and that was the same way she went to her new home. The trip to my farm was uneventful and she arrived, carrying my big dreams for a future champion of some sort within her belly. We renamed her Lady in fitting with her new role and my hopes for improving her cranky nature.

Xanadu was born on October 12, 1980. Both surprise and disappointment were mine that morning when I found a straggly, black object in the stall with Lady. She wasn't due to foal yet and hadn't been moved to the spacious foaling stall. The object turned out to be a stud colt. That was disappointment number one. I had my heart set on a filly to improve my small band of broodmares. I already had Delight for my stallion, and I didn't need or want another. Disappointment number two was that he was far from looking like champion material. He was small, rather ugly, wet and dirty. I was surprised at his size. His dam was sixteen hands and so was his sire. He should have been bigger to my way of thinking. For show horses, big does seem to be better. A good big horse will beat a good small horse in the show ring almost every time.

Except for the material care his mother and he needed, I pretty much ignored the little black colt. When Xanadu was a month old, I decided I should teach him to stand tied. My theory on training a horse is the younger you train it, the better. Teaching an adult one-thousand-pound horse to do something is much harder than teaching one that weighs two hundred pounds. I tied a rope around the foal's belly and then passed the end through the foal's halter and wrapped it around a post. Still holding the other end of the rope, I stood back to observe. With this system the foal feels a pull around his belly just behind his front legs when he backs up. Usually he will pull back more and more, sometimes he will sit down, lie down or just continue to pull. This is a safer method than trying to tie a young horse by the halter alone, because he could hurt his little neck by pulling hard. It is not a method to use and leave; one need's to be close by to let go of the rope if the foal will not back off it and release the pull. Little Xanadu backed up; I held the rope tight; he felt the rope tighten, stopped, cocked a hind leg and then dozed off. I was immensely impressed. I tried it again the next day with the same results. This turned out to be Xanadu's way of doing things— he looked the situation over and then calmly accepted it. I didn't have plans for the colt except to hold off gelding him, as his quiet nature and improving good looks made me wait.

By the time he was two and ready to ride, I decided he was so easy to work with, it would be foolish to either sell or geld him. At this point, although I showed my horses, I was not totally immersed in it. I still loved trail riding in the state parks and riding on the farm. I did, however, want a safe horse. I'd had enough of being dumped by ones with too much energy, nervousness or phobias. I decided since he was still a stallion, and possibly could be a handful to break, I'd send him away to be started under saddle, and then I would finish his training.

At this point I was becoming quite attached to him. There is something very special about a horse you can trust. I had a friend who lived close to Goshen who raised and trained show-quality Quarter Horses. I sent him to her. Shelia remarked he was one of the quietest and most sensible horses she had ever worked with, but there was one exciting event neither of us will ever forget.

Shelia had turned Xanadu out for his play time in her pasture and she watched as he took off bucking, leaping in the air and running full out—right up to a four foot fence he had not seen. It was either crash or jump. He jumped. Shelia saw him clear it easily and cleanly. Neither Shelia nor Xanadu could believe what just happened. Then the fun began for Xanadu as he cavorted through people's lawns, stopping occasionally for something to eat. It was not fun for Shelia as she chased him from one neighbor's garden to another, with lawn turf flying, but it all ended safely. Xanadu's ability to jump was filed away in my mind, but I didn't have any intention of ever putting it to use.

Stallions are nearly always separated from the females to avoid unplanned breeding as well as commotion. However, Xanadu had been such a gentleman around the other horses that after I weaned him, I left him with my little herd of mares. I was sure when they came into heat there would be some goings-on I would observe, and then I'd take the young stallion away until the mares went out of heat. I'd been breeding mares with Delight, and there was always lots of hubbub. Snorts, squeals and rowdy behavior were common. As the horses went out every morning and came in at night, I kept a watchful eye on them. I was sure I'd see something happen in the morning when they were all put out together, but it was always peaceful and quiet.

While Xanadu was away for training, I had the chance to sell Ebony, one of my mares, to some family friends in Ontario, Canada. I began to question myself about the mares, thinking it certainly was strange that I'd not seen anyone in heat for some time. Along with the many veterinarian tests that had to be done on the mare traveling into Canada, I had her pregnancy checked as well. Much to my surprise she was in foal. I couldn't believe Xanadu had pulled this off without my being aware of a darn thing. Apparently he was as quiet a soul in his amorous activities as in his riding. Next I had Missy checked and she was also pregnant.

When Xanadu returned from saddle training I returned him to the same pasture with the same mares. As soon as Xanadu entered the pasture with the mares, he went berserk. He singled out poor old one-eyed Missy and charged after her with mouth open, teeth showing and fire in his eyes. I just stood there and watched, horrified. This was the gentle, little horse I loved and now he was crazy. He chased Missy around and around the field. She was rather heavy in foal and on one of the turns around the pasture, Missy fell down heavily on her side.

By this time, fire was coming out of *my* eyes. On the next trip around the pasture Xanadu came close by the barn gate and as I swung it open, he peeled through. I shut it quickly behind him; after he made a round of the pen, he headed back to the pasture and found the gate closed. He was as mad as any horse I had ever seen. I left him there and went to see Missy. She had gotten back on her feet and although she had some scrapes, she seemed fine. Several days later she developed a big hematoma on the front of her chest which resolved over a couple of weeks. The foal was safe and born on the expected date.

Why Xanadu acted that way is yet a mystery to me. The conclusion I came to was that it was similar to a conquering male lion coming into a new pride that kills all the existing cubs so the females will be receptive to the new king and have his offspring. Xanadu sensed the presence of a competitor within Missy's belly and maybe he forgot that Missy was having his foal; maybe he thought he had to prove himself again. There are lots of maybes, but no one I ever talked to had a definitive answer as to why a gentle soul of a stallion would turn into a renegade with the same band of mares he'd left only a month before. This obviously put an end to his pasture days with other horses. From now on he would live his life separated from other horses, being with them only to breed or to be ridden in their company. It was going to be a new life for my little black stallion.

CHAPTER TEN

A Champion

It was new for me to have a horse I could ride while remaining relaxed. The Arabian horses and most of the other Walkers had some spook in them which wasn't good for my bad back, so having something dependable was a joy. Whether it was a cement truck roaring down the road, or a deer jumping out of the bushes right under our noses, Xanadu never came unglued. He was always willing to try different things; his attitude was priceless. Riding became really fun, and I fell in love with this little horse. Hal approved of my having a horse that was safe. He was busy, not much involved with the horses, but he did expect to come home to a wife with all her parts in the correct place.

The girls and I had just gotten into exhibiting our horses when I showed Xanadu as a yearling. Later, I showed him under saddle. He placed best in Western classes as his easy-going attitude towards everything suited Western riding the best. He placed in English-type classes where the horses are supposed to be more animated, but in his whole career, he only got one blue ribbon in that division. I tried him in Trail classes where the horse and rider navigate obstacles, such as crossing a bridge, going over water simulated by a big tarp, opening and closing gates while on the horse, ground tying and any other interesting and challenging activity the show committees can devise. He loved and excelled in trail.

By now I knew Xanadu would remain a stallion and he and Delight would share the mares coming to be bred. But he'd also be required to go to the shows, be a gentleman and mind his own business with mares around him, some perhaps in heat, and still perform in his show classes. He was totally excellent and above reproach at the shows. The only problem I had was at home.

We always had some mares and geldings boarded at our farm. Xanadu absolutely insisted on keeping his eagle eye on all the horse happenings, and it made his workouts and even trail rides difficult. He worked fast and lost his gait as he gawked at the other horses, sometimes neighing to them. He couldn't keep his mind on what he was doing. I resorted to riding him first thing in the morning before I turned out any other horses. He was perfect then. He knew where they all were and what they were doing, and he was happy. I think he actually enjoyed being at a show and away from the barn, because it gave him a rest from worrying about what the rest of the horses were doing. Being a herd sire was taxing work for my little stallion.

After going to a few shows and getting a blue ribbon in the model class where the horse is judged on appearance and conformation, I decided to participate in the Tennessee Walking Horse Breeders' and Exhibitors' (TWHBEA) Versatility Program. The versatility program was developed for horse and rider to showcase abilities other than ring work. Points are garnered at different shows and kept by the TWHBEA office. A High Point could be achieved in any of the divisions, or one could work toward a loftier goal of an Adult (or Youth) Versatility Championship, or go even further and work toward a Supreme Versatility Championship. Each required a prerequisite number of points earned in several different divisions such as Halter, English, Western, and Trail Class. Earning the Supreme Championship required even more total points plus points in additional more difficult categories, such as Hunter over Fences (hmmm), Driving to Cart, Western Riding, Barrels, and Pole Bending.

A number of model points were required, and I didn't know how Xanadu would stack up against bigger, more elegant horses. I was afraid getting the qualifying model points might prove too difficult. Xanadu was a great, little horse, but even I would not call him elegant. Yet after winning the blue ribbon in that first model class, I began to think we just might be able to win an Adult Versatility Championship. I sent in for my Point Book and we were off and running.

From the very beginning, Xanadu favored the Trail Classes. Since he loved them so much, he was easy to teach. He quickly learned to move his body inches one way or the other, back or forward to negotiate an obstacle. I always talked to my horses and soon found it was making an impression on Xanadu. I'd say, "Okay now, let's do the mail box." Very soon he associated the word "mail box" with getting close to it and standing still. This came in handy when we had to do a trail class in an especially noisy inside arena. The mail box was on the rail and people were hanging over the arena fence directly beside the mail box, watching the horses. It didn't look like a mail box obstacle to him, but because I told him it was, we did the job reasonably well, while many of our competition failed badly.

Most training hints tell you not to let your horse anticipate your signals especially in trail obstacles, but Xanadu had so much fun working them we developed a real partnership. In most of the classes, the other contestants and their horses were grouped about the arena, waiting their turns. If Xanadu could see the horses working the obstacle, he stared intensely. It took no imagination to guess he was planning how to work them better!

The only time we both fell flat on our faces was at a show in Milwaukee. That year had been the most exciting year in trail competition for us. Except for one very close reserve ribbon, we'd been undefeated. I was proud and very sure he would be impressive in Milwaukee. Then disaster struck. The show personnel decided to hold the trail class in the warm-up barn because the regular arena was too muddy.

Xanadu entered the barn and literally fell over the first obstacle, then proceeded to make a mess of the rest of them. He was totally unprepared for the class to be held in the warm-up area. It was a rather dark space between two rows of empty stalls—actually a very wide aisle which worked well for warming up horses before the ring classes, but wasn't a real arena. Since Xanadu had been using that area for warm up, I could see his mind wondering what in the blazes all that stuff was doing in there.

My favorite trail class that year was in Wilmington, Ohio. Ohio contestants were serious about their versatility events and were exceptional competitors. The eleven horse trail course had many interesting and difficult obstacles. Xanadu worked them like a pro and we won the class. Because of those points, that year found him TWHBEA Versatility High Point Trail Horse.

CHAPTER ELEVEN

That's Show Biz

One of my fondest memories with Xanadu will always be riding in the 1985 McDonald's Christmas Parade in Chicago on December first. ABC covered the event and Oprah Winfrey was one of the Chicago WGN commentators. When asked if I wanted to participate, it never entered my mind Xanadu couldn't be as perfect a parade horse on the streets of Chicago as he was in the shows. The horses and their riders used the theme of *Plantation Life* which depicted the era of the beginnings of the Tennessee Walking Horses. Riders and handlers portrayed planters, southern beaus and belles and a Confederate officer. I wore a costume with long-flowing legs which allowed me to sit astride Xanadu.

It rained most of the night before and continued that morning. We riders changed into our costumes in a horse trailer, and the horses were kept inside their trailers as long as possible to stay warm and dry. When the time came to be escorted to Wacker Drive, our staging area, we left our relative comfort and mounted up in some pretty dismal weather. It was a cold blustery December day with a nasty wind blowing off Lake Michigan. Chicago was living up to its name of the Windy City.

I had tried to dress warmly with long underwear and many layers, but by the time I got all this on, I could hardly bend my arms to hold the reins. While we were waiting for our turn to enter the parade, a magnificent six-horse hitch of black Percheron horses strode by, their heads high, noses snorting and their heavy hooves clacking loudly on the concrete. These large draft horses stood at 18 hands high and weighed nearly a ton each. Xanadu quickly turned around to head for Indiana and home. It was then it dawned on me Xanadu would be facing numerous new situations—sights and sounds, smells and demands—that might cause problems. Was he really ready for this?

Fortunately for us, it stopped raining and our six-horse group of Tennessee Walkers proceeded in the parade with no problem, coping with loud marching bands, big balloons and large noisy crowds.

At the parade's end, each horse and rider had to make their way back to the trailers parked on Wacker Drive. Half the street was blocked off; the other half had the usual Chicago traffic zooming by. As Xanadu and I flat walked down the street, a noisy, smelly city bus passed just feet from our side. I almost could have reached out and touched it. Xanadu acted as though this was an everyday occurrence to him, even though *I* was a bit nervous. At a busy intersection a person connected with the parade stopped traffic for us. I think I got a bigger thrill out of navigating that final city street than riding in the parade.

It was freezing cold by then and the snow was starting to fall. We loaded up and started home. My daughter, Michal, had taken time off from college at Indiana State to go with me and on the way home we drove into a blowing snowstorm. It was a bad enough storm that one of the parade participants wasn't able to make it home that night because of impassable roads in Wisconsin. We were extremely glad to reach home safe and sound. That weekend is a memory I will always warmly recall.

The next winter, I was asked by a local Elkhart dress shop if I had a horse that could be used in their spring bridal advertisement in the *Elkhart Truth Bridal Supplement.* Well, of course I did! I was sure Xanadu would love being a star. We practiced by dragging around a king-sized sheet draped all over him. The wedding dress was very expensive, and I didn't want to take the chance of causing it damage. The wind whipped the sheet around Xanadu's head and under his legs; he was not at all upset. I was sure we were ready for the big event. For spring clothing advertisements, the ads are shot in the late winter, so as luck would have it, it had to snow right before the scheduled shoot. The ground had been bare; now it had a least an inch of snow. The photographer decided to have the model sit on Xanadu and drape the gown over him.

Well, I wasn't worried. After all, we had practiced. Trouble was we hadn't practiced a big white blob getting *on* his back. Xanadu apparently felt dragging such a contraption was fine, but on top of him? He shied and jostled to get that billowy thing away from him. After about the sixth try, the model wasn't too sure about this anymore and the store manager was even less sure. All the while I was muttering, "He's *never* been like this before!"

Luckily, Xanadu finally decided there was just a person in the white blob and not some unknown monster, and he settled down and behaved. Maybe he saw his chance of being a celebrity fading fast. After all that, they decided that the white dress on the white snow background just didn't have the effect they wanted, so they scheduled another shoot. This time the model stood beside Xanadu on a sheet to protect the dress. They were afraid he would stand on the dress, and after what happened on the previous shoot I kept my mouth shut. But he didn't budge, and they were suitably impressed. The model had a fancy, white, open parasol to hold, and even that didn't bother him in the least.

Then the photographer and store manager—who obviously knew nothing about horses—started suggesting poses, and the now cold model started waving the parasol around Xanadu's head. I winced and bit my tongue but refrained from rushing up to give any suggestions. Xanadu held firm in his pose, a perfect model. Finally it was all over and the ad ran in the *Elkhart Truth*. They told me they had better shots of the horse, but in them the model didn't look good, so they went with the best shot of the model. Oh well, that's show biz.

CHAPTER TWELVE

Up and Over

Because Xanadu and I were doing so well getting our show points, I decided to go for the big one—The Supreme Versatility Championship. I dreamed Xanadu would become the first horse from Indiana to be thus honored and have his picture hang on the Wall of Fame in the Tennessee Walking Horse Breeders' and Exhibitors' Association building in Lewisburg, Tennessee, along with all the other Supreme Champions. I wasn't sure how far we would get in our endeavor, but in two years we'd gotten all the points we needed for Adult Versatility Champion. We now required points in our specialty event to achieve the Supreme Versatility Championship—*jumping*.

Xanadu's penchant for jumping and his raw ability would now be put to the test. It wasn't a matter of entering a class, jumping and getting a point; for each point earned one had to beat three horses. At Xanadu's first jump class, he and I were the only ones entered, so we wouldn't get a point, but I thought it would be good practice. It turned out to be more than just practice.

We came down the fence line at too fast a gallop, hooves pounding the ground as Xanadu, with way too much gusto, sailed over the small two-foot, six-inch jump as though it was five feet high, and dashed on to the next one. My heart was thudding in my chest and I don't think I was breathing. This was *not* the way we had done it at home! My bottom flew up off the saddle with each big jump and came back down with jolting back pain. At home it was fun. There Xanadu slowly cantered up to the jump and gently bounded over it. It was exhilarating—not heart stopping or painful. By the time we had finished the course, I was shaking in my new black riding boots, my poor lower back was hurting and I knew I couldn't compete him in the jumping classes.

It was plain to see that my nerves and back were not going to go for all this excitement. I needed a new rider. It would be the first time anyone other than I had ever shown him and I didn't know exactly how I felt about that. But if we were to proceed, if I was to stand a chance getting the coveted Supreme Versatility Award I so much wanted, I had to do it. Being relatively new at training horses and very new at jumping, I didn't recognize this first competitive jumping class for what it was: Xanadu was talking to me but I didn't hear. It would be a year later before I understood.

Mindy was a childhood friend of daughter Michal. She had no formal jumping training, but she jumped her Quarter Horse at local shows, was younger and braver than I was and was willing to take on the challenge of jumping Xanadu. Mindy and Xanadu received the first two points at two different Tennessee Walking Horse competitions, where the competitors were not professionally trained jumpers and all had similar problems and faults. After those shows, we had problems getting enough Walking Horses to compete against to garner points, so we needed to venture into the trotting horse world of jumping.

That would prove *much* more difficult.

Mindy took him to the Indiana and Michigan Open Hunter and Jumper shows, while Michal, Chessa and I continued on with our regular Walker shows. For several weekends this meant we couldn't go to the same event. It was sad for me to see Xanadu freshly bathed, hair trimmed, legs wrapped, new halter and blanket in place, load into Mindy's trailer and go without me. Mindy and Xanadu managed to get four more points mostly flying by the seat of their pants. Mindy was not schooled in jumping and Xanadu had started jumping just because I asked him. He'd always gotten me, and later Mindy, over the fence, no matter what it looked like or how we happened to approach it. He was gutsy and big hearted. He tried to do what we wanted and this would later get us into trouble.

Mindy and my horse were competing in classes with fences ranging from two feet, six inches to three feet. Their best accomplishment was getting second place out of nine horses in a green hunter class, giving us two points. The other points were picked up one-at-a-time at different shows. He showed in several classes, but only got one point for a weekend's work.

Several weekends he competed and came home without any points. These points were by far the most expensive and difficult of all the ones we ever earned.

Up until now I hadn't been free to go to any of the hunter shows, but finally our show schedule allowed me to go with them to Goshen, our home town. I was excited but apprehensive as well. Xanadu had started refusing fences, something he'd never done, and a lot of local people who knew him would be there to see him. He did his practice jumps perfectly outside the arena to warm up, and Mindy rode him around in the arena during lunch break to acquaint him with it. When his time came to compete I watched with my heart in my mouth. He cantered into the ring like a Western pleasure horse, looking at the ground and half asleep.

The duo made the customary preliminary circle and headed for the first obstacle. Xanadu's head flew up, his eyes widened and he put on the brakes, refusing to jump. He refused the second time and the third and we were disqualified. While I stood looking at the jumps before the class, I thought to myself that they looked awfully high. They were only three feet, but with just one white rail on a standard, it looked more like five feet. Solid jumps, or at least more rails between the posts, give the horse more to judge height and depth by. A single rail appears too airy underneath, giving the illusion of more height. I was really disappointed in Xanadu, and a little embarrassed. But more than that, I was worried.

I was able to go to the next jumping show. It wasn't a good day. Xanadu started out with two-foot and six-inch fences which he jumped okay, but his manner was hurried and anything but smooth. The next class had three-foot fences and oxers, which are two fences placed together making an extra wide jump. These were wide oxers and one was part of an in-and-out combination where the horse jumps one, lands and jumps the other one almost immediately. At this point, just looking at the obstacles he would face in a few minutes, I felt like taking him out and going home.

These fences didn't look like anything I thought he was ready for. Unfortunately I did not listen to my inner voice. Xanadu jumped the fences until he came to the oxer in-and-out combination. He absolutely refused, three times. We were also entered in the next class and they could be ridden back to back. Xanadu did the same thing except he was even more unglued before he ever got to that fence. I noticed a few of the other horses didn't like it either. It was hard to make the striding right to get over the oxer. I doubt Xanadu was physically capable of jumping it, and I am sure that is what he thought, too. It was obvious our jumping was in big trouble.

It wasn't difficult to find the problem. Xanadu, who was always willing to try, had been overfenced and frightened at the shows. At home we had worked on jumping fences that were two-foot and six inches to two-foot and nine inches. Our oxers were not as spectacular, high or wide. We jumped him in pre-green classes at shows, which worked out well, but because he seemed so willing, he'd been entered in classes with much more difficulty than he was prepared for. It had worked up to a point; it wasn't going to work any longer. It was July and we gave up showing him and started over with our training program. This was where I really understood the meaning of the saying "Haste makes waste." It would be much harder to achieve our goal now that Xanadu was frightened.

If I had only listened to Xanadu at that very first jump class where I rode him, I would have realized he needed much more training and conditioning. We jumped at home in a relaxed atmosphere. He knew his jumps and knew he could get over them. At the shows he knew bigger jumps were coming; it made him worried and frightened.

By now he had become apprehensive even over two-foot fences at home, so that was where we started. I felt like crying when I realized what I had done to my little horse with the heart of gold. The horses we were competing with now were serious about jumping. It wasn't a sideline for them as it was for us. I was out of my league and area of expertise. I needed help. It came in the form of a gifted instructor who was able to come to our farm and work with Xanadu.

Beth taught all kinds of riding from dressage to jumping. Mindy went back to college that fall and would graduate, so she wouldn't be available to show him any longer. Beth didn't want to compete Xanadu, but she agreed to help me work with him and look for another rider. All fall we trained over two-foot fences with the discipline of cantering a few yards, stopping, backing a few steps and striking off in the canter from a halt. This exercise strengthened him and helped round his canter and his jumps.

Because he had become frightened, he wanted to roar around at a fast gallop and blast over the jumps just to get it over with. He also had picked up the bad habit of landing in a cross canter. By winter he had improved a lot but still did not want anything to do with higher fences. Our plan was to build his confidence by lunging him over fences with no rider. Beth's favorite two comments about Xanadu were that he was "cute" and "cheery." It wasn't easy, but she taught him to jump four-foot fences on the lunge line with ease. She rode him over two-foot fences in the arena and he learned to change leads in mid air over the obstacle to go in another direction. Finally three-foot fences began to look small both to me and Xanadu.

That spring we were ready to hit the jumping circuit again, looking for our final two points, but we didn't have a rider. At the eleventh hour, Beth found one of her adult students, Cindy, who she thought would be able to place Xanadu at the correct takeoff spot, but otherwise leave him alone and let him jump. He had his own style and didn't want to be helped over the fences but getting to them was a different matter. This is where his easygoing manner got him into trouble.

He seemed to think he'd worry about the fence when he got there and too much of the time didn't place himself right, being either too far away or too close, making some of his jumps risky and unsightly. He was very willing to be placed, having learned to shorten or lengthen stride when asked,

spring 1988

but we needed a rider with a good eye. It comes easy for some but not for others. Cindy loved Xanadu at first sight, and she was gifted with a good eye for distances. She had been in a pony club as a teen, and she still enjoyed jumping, but her horse was now too old. The first show date was coming up in April, and Cindy had three days to get acquainted with Xanadu.

I think it speaks well of all our efforts, especially Cindy's, that Xanadu got a point at that first show. He was relatively calm. The course was inside and packed with jumps and sharp turns. The short warm-up session in the ring was exciting with horses all practicing at once. Xanadu had trouble with an in-and-out, but at least he did not refuse anything. In the first class he cross cantered and made some turns too wide, but luckily his second class was a repeat of the first one, and he had it down pat. He got a fourth, good enough for a point.

People were really interested that a Walking Horse could jump. As he came into the ring, I overheard people comment, "Here comes the Walker." We were greeted with smiles when we got our ribbon. Deciding Xanadu had done enough that day, we loaded him up and went home to plan for our eighth and final point.

Our next show was in an outside arena. I asked the lady in charge how high the jumps would be for the classes. The lowest ones would be three feet, the highest, four feet. I was a little apprehensive until I realized I was looking at them and they looked low. What a difference practice and training had made, even to me, the owner/spectator. Xanadu sailed over them with ease. He had some trouble with the turns, but did a fair job—we hoped. We had to get at least fourth place or there would be no point for us.

At the end of the class, our ears strained to hear the placings. We looked at each other nervously; I bit my lower lip to keep it from quivering and held my breath. So much was riding on this announcement. "And fourth place goes to number three, Xanadu, ridden by Cindy." Now if you think I stood there calmly, you are wrong! I had never cried at a show before, but I did then. Tears of joy and accomplishment slid down my cheeks. I knew how it felt to win the Kentucky Derby. I hugged Michal, Cindy, Beth, and everyone else in our group. Finally someone said, "Here is the one you should be hugging," and pointed to Xanadu. He stood there contentedly, hind leg cocked, ears flopped off to the side, wondering what all the fuss was about. His attitude seemed to say he had simply done his job. He had no idea what a wonderful horse I thought he was.

What had started out as a vague dream had now turned into a reality, and a little Tennessee Walking Horse who'd once cleared a pasture fence had been judged by a well-known and respected hunter-jumper judge and found worthy.

Xanadu *was* the first horse from Indiana to win the Supreme Versatility Championship and his picture hangs on the Wall of Fame in the TWH-BEA building in Lewisburg, Tennessee. After winning his Championship, he was semi-retired and we concentrated more on trail riding and breeding mares. For Xanadu life was good.

CHAPTER THIRTEEN

Xanadu the Lover

Xanadu was an easy breeding stallion. He had his usual ho-hum attitude about it, and I probably *could* have bred him with a shoestring, as the saying goes. Many were the times we had to breed a mare before we loaded him up to go to a show. After a stallion is allowed to breed, he usually doesn't mingle easily with horses at a show. His eyes wander, attention lapses, libido is noticeable, and he neighs to the mares—causing all sorts of uproar that does no good for the show and certainly keeps the stallion from doing well in competition. The usual way is to show, get a show record and then retire and breed mares. I didn't want to wait years to finish showing and then prove him as a sire; it would take too long. And Xanadu seemed more than able to keep his love life and show business life separate.

Xanadu was a lover; he wanted to take his time and there was lots of pillow talk involved. I became exasperated at his slowness in finishing the job and would tell him to hurry up. He'd look off to the woods, then back to the mare, talk to her some more and finally do the deed. He had a favorite color of mare. He loved the grey ones. There was far less time spent talking to a grey mare than other colored ones; his least favorite color was black. I thought this might be my imagination, but I read about one stallion who wouldn't breed his mares unless they were covered up with a blanket that made them appear to be his favorite mare color!

Xanadu was such a gentle stallion that it almost was his undoing. At one time he and Delight shared the breeding duties. Our barn was small so the stallions were kept on opposite sides of it. They couldn't see each other from their stalls, but there was no hiding the fact they both resided there.

One morning when I went to feed all the horses, I became aware that Xanadu was in Delight's stall with the stall door shut. This was certainly very curious. The first thing I noticed about Xanadu was that he was covered with dried sweat. His usual shiny, black coat was dirty and crusty. What in the world had happened? Then I noticed a big bloody bite on Xanadu's throat. He looked like he had run ten miles; he stood quietly in the stall with no desire to move even toward me.

I went to Xanadu's stall where the door was open, and there was Delight. He had dried sweat on him too, but unlike Xanadu, he was perky and pleased with himself. In piecing together what must have happened, I figured Delight had somehow gotten out of his stall and gone visiting. When he found Xanadu, he decided to eradicate him from the breeding line up. By fussing at Xanadu through the stall gate, it somehow opened and the fight was on.

Xanadu protected himself even when Delight went for his jugular; how long they battled in a horse stall, I don't know. Delight emerged the victor obviously, but Xanadu fought well enough to stay alive. How the stall door got shut with Xanadu inside and Delight outside is another mystery, but probably one that had saved Xanadu from further injury.

After that fiasco, we all made double sure that the stallions' stall doors were tightly locked with new and stronger fasteners. Delight fell from my favor because of his fighting, although what he had done was natural instinct. He thought survival of the fittest worked in a small breeding establishment the same as on an open range, but it was a dangerous trait in my mind and when the opportunity arose, I found Delight a new home in Idaho, keeping only Xanadu, the gentle lover.

CHAPTER FOURTEEN

The Ending of an Era

Delight had gone to a new home; Xanadu was the only stud, and my thoughts turned to having another stallion. A quiet one, but one with more excitement to his gait. While traveling to Tennessee with Carol, I met some very friendly and helpful people who were well known for breeding fine colts and always had some top sellers at the fall horse sales. One of them contacted me about a colt by Pride's Generator, a very prominent sire. I didn't go see the colt, but I had a friend who was in the area do so for me. She thought I should buy him.

When he arrived at New Acre, I was very disappointed. He was a pretty yearling, but not the caliber of colt I had seen these breeders present. In actuality, I guess I couldn't have afforded one of those top colts, but this horse didn't live up to my expectations. For a second stallion, I had wanted one that would be flashier and better gaited in the show ring. But the deal had been struck, and I couldn't afford yet another stallion. I hoped he might still work out in the long run.

I named the new colt Generator's Galahad and started his training under saddle that fall. He and Xanadu shared the barn with no conflict; I was able to show him and breed him to several mares. It turned out, I learned quite a bit from Galahad.

As a trainer I was always open to new techniques and tools to improve my methods. I wasn't really fond of snaffle bits which are considered to be gentle, having no shanks for any torque, just a mouth piece with rings attached to the side for the bridle and reins. I'd always used a short, gently curved shank bit for breaking and riding and never had any problems, but since I was ready to learn new things, especially if it was better for my horse, I got a snaffle bit. Perhaps my distrust of snaffle bits was slightly buried in my subconscious, as I remembered that Peggy, a childhood horse, ran away with one in her mouth.

On our family farm in Pennsylvania we had raked our hay with Smokey, my first and very gentle, small work horse. One day in my inexperienced sixteen-year-old ignorance, I had decided to take his work-mate Peggy. Why should my sweet Smokey have to do all the work? The problem with my plan was that Peggy was nowhere near as safe or sweet as Smokey. When I finally got her hitched to the hay rake and climbed onto the seat, Peggy took off running as fast as she could back to the barn. She was frightened out of her wits by the clanking rake. Even if I had the toughest bit in the world, I likely could not have stopped her panicked gallop, but with a snaffle, I had no chance at all. I ended up falling off and hitting my head on a big rock, getting a headache and stitches.

Galahad was broke and somewhat trained, so I anticipated no problem as I started out on my ride around the hay field with the new bit. My mistake was going away from the barn into areas where anything might spook a horse. If I'd stayed in the riding arena where the horse felt comfortable, I would probably have had a safe ride with my new snaffle.

We had gone all the way around the field and had started on the second round when something unfathomable to me scared the dickens out of Galahad, and he took off running. The best and sometimes only time to get a runaway stopped is within the first seconds before the horse gets up to speed. With the gentle bit, the horse had me at a disadvantage. Galahad couldn't go in a straight line to the barn because of a creek with trees along it, so he began lapping the field. After the first few hundred yards and some muttered expletives I am ashamed to admit I uttered, my words became a prayer for providential help.

I tried my hardest to use the pulley method of stopping a horse that is running out of control. The idea is to pull on the left rein with your left hand as close to his mouth as you can reach, and pull his head around to make him run in circles. You use your right arm and hand against his neck for leverage to help turn his head to the left, or you could do the same to the right. I am a relatively strong woman and at that time was quite a bit younger, but try as I might, there was no way I was getting him to turn his head and run in smaller and smaller circles until he gave up. About the time

I was sure I was going to be dumped and contemplated bailing off, he stopped still. This was another mystery which proved when dealing with animals, one truly can have no idea what is going through their minds.

Galahad came the rest of the way home, gentle as could be, but I was shaking in my riding boots and never again used a snaffle outside the arena.

Galahad had some quirkiness to him. Before I gelded him, he did something that if I hadn't seen the results with my own eyes, I wouldn't have believed it. Our stud pens had ten foot buffer zones around them so the stallions couldn't get right up to another horse across the fence. Galahad was in one of these next to a mare in another pasture. One morning I went out to feed and found Galahad in with the mare. I just stood there, looking in disbelief at the fences. There was a hole dug under each of them with piles of dirt on his side of both fences. He had dug a hole just barely big enough to slip his body under, not once but twice. That would have been one for Amazing Videos shown on television. I wish I had seen it.

In 1988, we built a large barn with twenty stalls and a large inside riding arena. Xanadu moved into the new barn with great aplomb. He was eight years old and king of all he surveyed. The next two years were good ones. I rode him at least once a day, sometimes twice. He had his mares to breed, and we still showed him now and then just for fun. We had nothing to prove, but he had his admirers, and I loved competing with him.

Exhibiting a horse to cart was one of the Versatility Classes offered at our shows. I had never had a desire to sit behind a horse since Peggy's infamous runaway, but now I gave it serious thought. Xanadu would surely be safe, I could conquer a fear, and it would give us a new challenge. In due course I got a cart, harness and someone to help us get started. True to form, Xanadu carried it off as though he was an Amish buggy horse. I got a big thrill out of my new venture. I don't think I smiled any bigger the first time I rode Steamboat, the very first horse I ever rode, than I did the initial time I drove Xanadu.

We took the cart to a Wisconsin show in our four horse trailer; however, the vehicle took up the last horse slot, so we had to leave a horse at home. We won the driving class, the completion of another goal, but that was the only occasion we took the cart. I actually was brave enough to compete in the jumping class; it was the first time I showed him over fences since my first and too exciting exhibition ride at the very beginning of our jumping adventures. What a difference training had made. He was perfect, even to jumping the middle fence on a slight diagonal to make the smoothest round. He excelled in the trail class as well. That show was the final time I showed Xanadu. It was a bittersweet experience, but we exited the show circuit in triumph.

After Xanadu achieved the TWHBEA Supreme Versatility Award in 1988, I felt complete. We as a family had achieved a goal. Xanadu had been recognized as a national figure, and our New Acre Farm had expanded to include seventy-five more acres, a large new barn with twenty stalls and an inside riding arena.

Boarding horses for people on a larger scale was a new avenue to be pursued. Other people's horses would keep me occupied plus be more profitable. Now maybe I would enjoy my horses for pleasure. We still showed the mares, but it wasn't as hectic a show schedule as when we were promoting Xanadu.

As it turned out, this move away from showing Xanadu might have been necessary even if we hadn't planned it that way. Xanadu was now ten years old, and in that year he had some kind of a stallion personality change. Up to that point he had been very accepting of Galahad, the other stud, and all the horses on the farm, although he still wanted to know what each horse was doing. We tactfully bred Galahad to mares in an area which Xanadu could not see. He could watch all the pasture horses from his private paddock and he was content. One day, out of the blue, he charged his stall door with his mouth wide open, his front teeth bared and his ears flat back on his head, as another horse was led past. I was shocked. What had caused him to develop this nasty attitude? I would ponder that question for years, ask questions no one could answer, and finally came up with my own deduction.

I reasoned it was some sort of a male mid-life crisis, maybe triggered by some hormonal change. Xanadu did not perceive the other horses in the same fashion after that day. He always charged his stall when a horse was going by, hitting his open teeth so hard against our very solid stall fronts that I feared for his teeth's safety. It was an ugly and depressing sight. To protect his teeth, I wound very fine wire in and out of the bars and electrified it with a fence charger. The wire grounded out on the bars, but charged them at the same time. Xanadu got a nasty shock if he hit the bars which stopped him from injuring himself, but it also shocked us if we forgot to turn it off. I tried a roll-up bamboo curtain I could unroll before letting the horses in for feeding. All these things worked, but they were too much bother. In the end Xanadu won; he continued his stall charging.

Other things in our family were also changing. Through mutual friends in Pennsylvania, Hal and I met a young man who would enter our lives and become like a second son. His name was Bob and he was the same age as Sharon. Bob wanted to get his Bachelor's degree in business, and later his MBA. Hal suggested that he live with us on the farm, go to Indiana University at South Bend, and finish his schooling here. It was an auspicious idea that would have far reaching ramifications in later years.

Michal had just graduated from Indiana State with a degree in criminology and was hired by the Elkhart Police Department, soon becoming Elkhart's first woman K-9 Officer. Chessa was graduating from high school; It seemed we were all ready to begin something new. I felt fortunate that our show family had been able to stay together for such a long time. When Michal started college, I thought our showing adventures would end, but they didn't. We shared ten years together doing what we loved with our horses. I started thinking about retiring from the show ring.

A little sorrel colt was born in May that year on the Harlinsdale Farm in Franklin, Tennessee, home to the great Midnight Sun. I didn't know it yet, but that colt would change my life. I was about to open a powerful new chapter with my horses. One that would inspire more growth in me as a horsewoman and would change forever how I perceived them.

Michal and Lanzo

CHAPTER FIFTEEN

Mr. Macho

Xanadu was eight years old when he achieved the Supreme Versatility Award. Two years later, his breeding career had all but ended. We didn't ship semen so we couldn't reach far away mares, and the folks close enough to bring mares had already taken advantage of his genetic contribution.

Meanwhile, I was rethinking my goals. Having a stallion to promote at the horse shows was good business, but Xanadu and I had accomplished our goal. The time had come for him to retire, but what about me? Some days I thought I might enjoy less work; then again, I knew I would miss showing my horses. My daughters were starting out in a new part of their lives, but we still enjoyed showing, even if less frequently, and I still had a goal I hadn't yet achieved. I wanted a show horse that would be different from Xanadu— one that could get consistent top place ribbons in the rail classes which were judged on the Tennessee Walking Horse gait. This required a horse that had a bigger stride to his walk and more charisma.

I was getting along well with stallions, and since I was trying to run a breeding farm, my new horse should be another stallion. In 1990, our usual group of exhibitors consisted of my daughters, Michal, Chessa, and me. One of the shows on our summer circuit was held in Mason, Michigan, at the Ingham County fairgrounds. After we unloaded and bedded down our horses for the evening, we did the usual visiting with horse friends. The big talk was about a new two-year-old stallion Sherri, a trainer from Ohio, had in her show string. Her horses were always good, and they usually won those prized blue ribbons.

Sherri trained a lot of horses from Harlinsdale Farm, owned by Bill Harlan. His dad had owned Midnight Sun who stood at stud for years on the farm and whose grave can still be seen there. The Harlan family had been in the Tennessee Walking Horse business since 1935, breeding and owning numerous famous horses. Many of Sherri's horses-in-training were either owned by Mr. Harlan or by people who had purchased promising yearlings at their fall production sale. This latest buzz was about a stallion named Mr. Macho, owned by Mr. Harlan and scheduled to be shown in the Plantation two-year-old class.

Our Walking Horse classes are divided into three divisions according to the shoeing limitations or requirements. The Plantation division showed in a heavy shoe, similar to the showy gaited Saddlebred horses and the Lite Shod division in a much lighter shoe similar to regular pleasure horse shoes. The Trail Pleasure division had the same shoeing requirement as the Lite Shod horse but the Trail Pleasure horse was not expected to be as flashy in the show ring; he was to be more like a regular horse ridden on the trails. None of these divisions allowed the use of pads or chains.

I didn't have a Plantation horse to compete, so I could be in the audience and watch Mr. Macho in the first class of his career. As I had never seen the horse, I sat on the bleachers beside a friend who knew what he looked like. As the class entered the ring she pointed him out—a light sorrel with a reddish mane and a mixed tail of red and white. He had a small star on his forehead, and his attractive head was refined with small, nice-looking ears. He was striking in a young horse sort of way. He flowed around the ring with seemingly effortless grace. He was consistent in his footfalls, no short then long steps, no slowing down or speeding up. He was a vision to behold.

After the class, with Mr. Macho and Sherri winning the blue ribbon, Michal and I rushed to Sherri's stalls. I asked to see him and she opened his door for us. He was not nearly as imposing appearing as he had been in the ring. He was standing with a hind leg cocked, the way a horse rests when not lying down. He was rather indifferent to our presence, but that was all right. I liked the fact he was calm, not pacing his stall or calling to other horses and acting like an idiot stallion. I didn't know a lot about Walking Horse conformation at this phase of my life, but I instinctively knew he was built to walk. His body was all in balance. He was 15 hands tall, not a big horse, and being a young two-year-old, he wouldn't yet have a stallion's muscular body.

It was a ridiculous thing to do, but I asked Sherri if he was for sale and how much he would cost. She replied that he was for sale, but she thought someone in her training barn was interested in him. *Well, darn,* I thought, yet part of me sighed in relief. For I'd have looked pretty silly when she stated the price and I had to admit I couldn't afford him. It had been a nice dream anyway.

We went home from the show, but I couldn't get Mr. Macho out of my mind. I'd heard an interesting event that had sent him to Sherri in the first place. Every fall during and after the National Celebration which is the biggest show for Tennessee Walking Horses held in Shelbyville, Tennessee, there are many production sales showcasing the yearling horses from all the famous breeding stallions, many of which were former World Grand Champions. Harlinsdale Farm had such a sale.

Mr. Macho was included, but he had stuck his right front foot through one of the openings of his stall at the sale barn and cut his pastern area. He was removed from the sale and taken home. He would not be able to become a big lick show horse because the injury, even when healed, would not allow the use of chains in that area. But the pleasure end of the industry was starting to take hold, and Mr. Harlan sent him to Sherri to be trained for that division.

Days went on and I still couldn't forget that horse. Finally, I talked to my husband about him. Owning Mr. Macho was a dream not likely to come true. First and foremost was the question of money; all my other horses had been purchased for much less than any stallion of Mr. Macho's breeding and obvious abilities. The other hurdle was that he was being considered by someone else.

Hal and I talked, prayed, and came to the conclusion if somehow he was available to me, we'd take it as heavenly guidance and we'd buy him. If Mr. Macho was not available, I'd know another path lay somewhere ahead for me. Prayer was involved because I had been talking to God a lot about my having a supreme show horse for some time.

It was plain to Hal and me that God did have some sort of plan for our lives. There is no way one can live through a direct hit from a tornado, as we had in 1965, and not have faith that you are meant to be on earth for a reason. God had seen fit to bestow upon me a soul-deep love for animals, especially horses, and had set me on my path of sharing their lives. I was ready for the next phase, if there was to be one.

My previous foray into showing had been satisfying, but now my lofty goal was to compete at the top shows in our several state area and travel to Tennessee to the two biggest shows—the Celebration and the International and get top ribbons! Previous showings had been at smaller shows with only local competition. At the Celebration and International, top horses came from across the entire country to compete. I needed a special horse to accomplish this dream.

I called Sherri various times during those summer months, but no, Mr. Macho was still being considered by someone else. I called Mr. Harlan asking if he had another horse just like Mr. Macho. That question really couldn't be answered without a crystal ball, but he was sure he did and sent me the production sale brochure. I didn't know how to go about looking at yearlings from a brochure to pick out a winner. It would be much easier to pick one that I could see being ridden, not to mention already winning under saddle.

One day at the end of August, I got a telephone call from Sherri, telling me that if I wanted Mr. Macho, I could have him; the other people had backed out. I asked the price and took a deep breath. Yes, the price was high, but the decision had already been made for me by this turn of fate. Funds in hand, I wasted no time driving several hours to her stable in Ohio to take a final look at the horse and to ride him myself. This was the second time in my life I had seen him and the only time I had ridden him; I had to make a big decision. She was leaving for the Celebration in two days and I could own him now, or take the chance that someone would buy him at the show grounds, a very common place for horse transactions. I took the plunge. He had already been entered in the Plantation two-year-old class under Mr. Harlin's name and his name would appear in the show program, but I was fine with that. I would be recognized as the owner when the class was judged.

It was all coming together so fast it made my head spin. I had just purchased a fine horse and he was going to show at the Celebration, *The* Tennessee Walking Horse show of the year!

Sherri and her horses arrived at the Celebration grounds several days before the events started in order to get them rested and ready to show. Another possible scenario presented itself. What if I was offered more money than I'd paid for Mr. Macho? Other exhibitors, trainers and prospective buyers would see him. Sherri was well known. Should I sell my dream only a few days after I bought him? I contacted her and told her that if someone made an offer to buy him, she should let me know.

I couldn't answer the question of selling him by myself. I felt guilty having paid such a sum for a horse, and horses are known for dying when you least expect it, or getting career-ending injuries. Another wife and husband conference was needed. My dear, sweet husband listened to all my worries and then said, "I don't see why *you* can't have a great horse as well as anyone else." And that was that. I called Sherri back and told her I wouldn't sell him, no matter what. She later told me she had indeed received an offer of nearly double what I'd paid, but Mr. Macho was mine to keep.

I wasn't able to go to Tennessee and watch his performance, but I had someone video tape the class and call me as soon as it was over. When I answered the phone and heard the words, "He won!" my feet were floating somewhere off the ground. Mr. Macho had just been crowned the 1990 World Champion Two-Year-Old Pleasure Horse...shown by Sherri Szucs and owned by Rose Miller of Goshen, Indiana! My friend gave me the description of the class and the horse's performance—and the word awesome was used several times. I excitedly anticipated my new stallion's homecoming.

CHAPTER SIXTEEN

A Horse in Training

I renamed my new horse Praise Hallelujah, in homage to his sire Pride's Hallelujah and as credit to my faith in Divine guidance. His mother was sired by Pride's Gold Coin who was sired by the great Sun's Delight. Years down the road Praise Hallelujah would start his own line of horses—the Praise line.

All that winter, I enjoyed riding Hallelujah, Praise, or just H as he became known at the barn. He was wonderfully gentle for a stallion, which was very important to me. I had plans to put Hallelujah with a trainer the next spring because I realized I was not well enough versed in show horse training to make Praise Hallelujah the best he could be. In the spring of 1991, I sent him to Ralph, a trainer near Indianapolis, Indiana.

Having a horse with a trainer was very different from my usual horse life. Instead of washing our show horses, loading them and all the horse show necessities into our trailer and heading to the show, Michal, Chessa and I drove in a car to Hallelujah's first competition as a three-year-old with our new trainer. We stayed clean. No more grooming or messy black stuff to apply to beautify his feet and consequently get on us. Ralph and his wife Betsy did it all.

This was great. I could pet my horse and I was allowed to give treats–in his feed tub, not by hand. Hallelujah's tail was kept in a tail bag so pieces would not break off, and it grew to touch the ground. The whiskers on his muzzle and the hair in his ears were trimmed to perfection. I trimmed my own horses, but I was not the greatest with ear trimming. My trim jobs always left errant hairs that were visible upon close inspection. Yes, it was exciting to have a horse in training. It was so exciting in fact, the first show I forgot to pack my show clothes in the car! Betsy went among their acquaintances at the show and borrowed different items from them for me to use.

Watching Ralph and Hallelujah in the ring was even more exciting. He had Hallelujah traveling around the arena with a flair I had never seen. He was three years old and more mature than when he competed with Sherri. His body was becoming more muscular with all the riding, and he carried himself with more presence. He knew he was a stallion and something to be reckoned with. He had the Look of Eagles. Wow, was I proud.

Ralph showed him in the Open classes, and I showed him in some Amateur classes which excluded the trainers. It was definitely different not having my horse at home to practice riding. I had nothing that compared to him, nothing that could prepare me for his energy and high spirits. Horse trainers have different methods of schooling their horses. Ralph's system was great for him, but scared the liver out of me. Hallelujah was kept in a stall and fed lots of nutritious feed, not the least of which was high powered protein grain.

This wasn't at all unusual for a show horse. Aside from generating energy, the horses are safer in a stall than running free to fall down, step in a hole, run into a fence or any other disaster horses seem to make for themselves. My show horse in training lived a very different life from my pasture kept pleasure show horses. Hallelujah's only exercise was when Ralph rode him and believe me, Hallelujah was raring to go!

Ralph also rode with long spurs, which he seldom needed to use; his horses knew they were there and what they would be used for. Since the horse stayed in his stall, his hooves were allowed to grow longer than they would if he was a pasture horse. The longer foot and the heavier shoe, gave more animation. Riding Hallelujah while he was in this frame of mind was akin to driving a Ferrari on rain-slicked roads without prior experience in the vehicle. It was at the same time exhilarating and frightening. Nevertheless, that first year with Ralph, I had some great rides and won many blue ribbons.

Although Hallelujah was a young stallion, he never acted like one at the shows; he was a perfect gentleman. He was, however, full of himself. I understood that to get a horse animated in a more natural way, Hallelujah had to be almost bursting at the seams. He was not working out of pain; he

The Look of Eagle
Photo by Terry Young

was working out of very high spirits. The horse always knew who was riding him. He performed with much more flash and enthusiasm with Ralph in the saddle than when I rode him–which was a very good thing.

Amateur classes were for the non pro-riders. When I showed him, I was with others who either trained their own horses, or rode a professionally-trained horse as I did. We were all in the same boat with our horses, so the fact he was less animated in those classes was all right. We did very well for ourselves. I was amazed how Hallelujah seemed to take care of me in the class. He appeared to know where to go to get between or pass horses. He had a lot of power and he could go faster than a lot of my competition. The judges liked the speed, providing that the horse did not fall apart in his gaits. He knew the call of the different gaits: flat walk, then faster to the running walk. He looked neither right nor left; he just did his job. Although I didn't sit there like a passenger, Hallelujah knew what he was doing and I loved it.

At large shows, the horse that wins a class is allowed to do a victory lap. When the judge has completed his assessment of the horses, they are called in to line up in the middle or an end of the arena. As the placements of the class are called, horse and rider go to get their ribbon. First place is almost always called and given first. At the shows which have a photographer, the winner stands in front of the show banner or sign and has a picture taken. While this is taking place, the rest of the placings are called and those horses and riders pick up their ribbons and leave. If there are just a few horses in the class, they are gone quickly, leaving the winner standing alone. When the ring is cleared of other horses, the winner makes his victory ride.

Praise Hallelujah *hated* making victory passes. He saw it as a punishment for being first. He had to wait and be the last to leave. Horses are herd animals and they would rather be together. Hallelujah got more and more nervous as the horses left. As his career went on, some days it would be next to impossible to get a standing picture with the blue ribbon.

There was much fanfare for the winner. The music got loud, the announcer called the horse's and rider's names as they started the victory lap and with much style and aplomb the winner rode out of the arena. Well, Hallelujah wanted none of it. The music and loudspeaker just intensified his desire to leave. He even gave Ralph some excitement a time or two. As the horse does his lap, the photographer gets an action shot of the winner. Those pictures are normally spectacular as the horse is performing at his utmost.

My first victory pass was the most frightening thing I had ever done involving a horse since Peggy ran away with me pulling the hay rake. How I managed to stay on is a miracle. I got back at my daughter, Michal, for all the grey hairs she had ever given me, by having her watch Hallelujah and me do victory passes over the ensuing years. It was alarming enough that I mentioned to an old trainer that it almost made me not want the blue. His comment was, "Forget the victory pass; *get the blue!*" Many times that is just what we did. Got the blue and left…

Some horses love the victory passes. They know they are on parade and they are proud. I have had some of Hallelujah's daughters do marvelous victory laps. Done on a horse who enjoys them, it is a very heady experience. Nevertheless, till the day he retired, Hallelujah by no means got into the spirit of that victorious moment.

CHAPTER SEVENTEEN

Praise Hallelujah

R alph always went to the National Celebration in Tennessee. Praise Hallelujah would be going, and this time so was I. I'd missed seeing him as a two year-old with Sherri, but not this time!

Ralph went earlier and showed my horse the last Sunday before the Celebration at the fifth annual Pleasure Walking Horse Flatshod Celebration in Lebanon, Tennessee. Many of the Celebration contestants were in the area to test their horses before the big show. Ralph and Hallelujah pulled off an awesome win in a class of eighteen entries in the Three Year Old Class. My hopes soared for his showing well at the Celebration, even though I knew the class would have even greater competition.

The first Celebration classes for my horse were during the day. The large class of three year olds entered the indoor Calsonic Arena one by one and Ralph and Praise Hallelujah were among the first entries. I sat in my seat, hardly breathing. They looked good—really good. Hallelujah was lifting his front legs, bending at the knees with his forearm level with his body. That was great lift. His rear stride was solid and even, no sign of pace, no lack of flow. His long neck was held high, his chin tucked just right and his nodding headshake was more than ample. Hallelujah's head shake was one of his claims to fame. Many horses had little or none. But would it be good enough to win the Three-Year-Old Championship?

In my eyes, it was a wonderful effort. I was sure they had every chance of another national title, The Three Year Old Pleasure World Championship. First place was called and it went to a little mare from California. Second place went to a Tennessee horse. Third place went to Hallelujah and

Ralph. I was disappointed, but my horse and I were in the big league now and the game was played a little differently. One took chances and took your knocks. If one didn't have the stomach for losing he had better hang it up and quit. These shows were unlike the smaller local ones in which Xanadu and my other show horses had competed. This class was preserved on video tape and watching it time and again, even after I became a judge myself, I still think Hallelujah had as much chance to win as the two who placed above him. The three-judge system made it complicated and politics gave it another twist. I would have to content myself with the fact that Ralph and Hallelujah had received one first-place vote of the three cast. It was not a bad achievement; after the first blush of disappointment, I was pleased.

The twosome competed again in the Gentlemen Class which required the canter. Many young horses do not canter. The Three-Year-Old class didn't require that gait. The winner was a mare from California. This time Hallelujah was up against matured or aged horses, most of whom had lots of experience and blue ribbons. Second place was called, then third. We got the fourth place tie. This time I was very happy.

Ralph asked me if I wanted to show my horse in the Amateur Rider Championship. Gulp! Yes I did, but my stomach twisted in knots. I had taken my show clothes (just in case), but I'd planned on being the proud owner who applauded Ralph. I turned to my companions for an opinion. My daughter Michal and another good horse friend, Pat, had gone to Tennessee with me for this show. They, along with Ralph and his wife, encouraged me to do it, asking, "How many times will you get the opportunity to actually show at the National Celebration in the big oval outside ring?" This was true; it was a chance of a lifetime. But was I actually prepared?

During the whole summer season, I rode Hallelujah in Amateur classes at local shows held in Indiana, Michigan, Ohio and Kentucky. It had been difficult for me even in those shows because I didn't know my horse that well. When you can ride a horse every day, you know his flaws and his strong points. You fit together like a hand in a glove. With a horse in training, the trainer rides every day and you, the owner, ride at shows or when you go to visit your horse. I think some trainers cringe at the thought of their amateur owner showing or riding the horses and undoing much of their schooling. That is the difference between amateur and open classes. Amateurs are not expected to do as good a job as the trainers, and with few exceptions, they don't. This would be a plus in my showing Hallelujah at the Celebration in the Amateur Championship. I might have a better chance of a top ribbon than if Ralph showed three-year-old Hallelujah in the Open Championship against other trainers on aged horses.

It took me two days to decide I would compete. The championships are held at the end of the show and in the large outside arena. The show was ten days long so I had ample time to sweat the decision. In due time, Hallelujah and I, along with Ralph, entered the warm-up area waiting to have my horse inspected before entering the ring. After inspection I rode him at a walk in the small enclosure to keep his muscles limber. I looked around at the horses warming up and already felt defeat. These people were more experienced; most of the horses were awesome. I was getting more and more nervous. Finally the class was called and we all entered.

I kept telling myself this was just another horse show, nothing to be anxious about; but in fact, it *was* a big deal. It was the biggest show of the year and in the country for Tennessee Walking Horses. Here was my chance to do the very thing I had dreamed of—to have an awesome horse and compete at the highest level, but it came sooner than I expected. Fear crept in.

I know Ralph wanted us to do well. It is nerve-wracking for a trainer to stand on the sidelines and watch. As Hallelujah and I entered the ring, Ralph swatted my horse's butt with a short whip. Oh boy, *now* we were up in the bridle, picking those front legs up as high as when Ralph showed him, but it had taken me unaware. I lost my balance a little and clutched the reins tighter as Hallelujah strode those first steps into the big ring. But my surprise didn't phase this extraordinary horse's stride. The momentum of that entrance began to die out, and by the time we reached the end of the first long side, I felt more in control of my horse. We could do this. We *could* do this. All of a sudden I felt a rush of pride, not in myself, but in Hallelujah who seemed to act as though this really was just any old horse show. He wasn't nervous and he was listening to me. Most of my fear was gone, and in its place was a feeling of reverence and gratitude to that Higher Being who had seen fit to bless me with this awesome stallion.

It takes awhile for twenty or so horses to enter a ring and if you are one of the first, as we were, you either have to stop and stand while the rest come in, or navigate through the ones still entering which is considered bad form. I pulled Hallelujah up and waited for the rest to enter. When all the class was in and we started going again, Hallelujah was not as animated as he had been, but there was a lot of noise from the music and people yelling, and I still had some butterflies in my stomach.

Each time we passed Ralph on the side of the ring, he yelled at me to get after Hallelujah and make him flashier. We were doing just fine, I thought. Hallelujah felt awesome to me, but Ralph was right, too; if we wanted a good placement, Hallelujah needed spark. Another consideration was that many of these professionally trained pleasure horses had been sored. Competing with them required that Hallelujah do his utmost. Pumped for a ribbon, I pushed my heels into my horse's side to go with more pizzazz. An instant later I recalled that Ralph and I rode differently; I have always used my legs on the sides of my horses and Ralph never did. In that same instant Hallelujah cantered! Oh gosh, how perfectly awful.

I am a good rider and had competed Hallelujah all summer with great results, but the pressure was on at the Celebration. I felt like crawling under my saddle. Ralph probably turned green. Going in the other direction on the reverse, the same thing happened. As I pushed him up into the bridle, he cantered again. This was worse than awful. I finished the class, mad as I could be—mad at Ralph for telling me to push the horse and not allowing me to ride him the best I could in my own way, mad at Hallelujah for cantering, and most of all mad at myself for the miscue. As I sat on my horse in the lineup, waiting for the placement of the class, I was thinking that I might as well have taken the one-hundred-dollar entry fee and thrown it away. I was furious and embarrassed.

I barely listened to the results, so I nearly fell off Hallelujah when his name was called for ninth place out of the ten that were given. The payback was an even hundred. I was still so upset when we exited the ring that I had angry words with Ralph—not the best thing to do to with a trainer. Before the show was over, we had more or less made peace, but I was not sure what to do with Hallelujah for the next year. I'd been training and showing my own horses for thirteen years. Maybe I just wasn't cut out to have someone else train my horse and tell me how to ride him.

Later, when looking at the five judges' cards posted from that class, I saw that the two judges who didn't see us break gait into the canter had given us a fourth and a fifth. Another judge gave us a tenth place tie. While that was enough to give us the ninth placing, I always will wonder what the results would have been if we had not blown our chance by making such a big error, not once but twice. Having the opportunity to show a horse at the

Celebration was huge for a country gal who had always trained her own horses. The anger I felt was not because I did not get the blue ribbon —that was a near impossibility—or even place in the top five which would have been a significant achievement. Rather it was because I hadn't ridden my horse the best that I could but had ridden to please the trainer instead of following my own intuition and had ended up pleasing neither of us.

I had a lot to think about on the way home. On the one hand, I loved training my own horses. I knew them better by doing all the riding myself. On the other hand, I realized I wasn't ready to take on the momentous and daunting task of training and showing a stallion of Praise Hallelujah's caliber. This was a whole new life I had before me. I was very unsure of my next move.

CHAPTER EIGHTEEN

Tennessee Walking Horse Shows

In 1991, as the show year progressed with Hallelujah in training with Ralph, I began to notice something about the pleasure show horses. I showed my other pleasure horses in northern Indiana, Michigan, Illinois and Wisconsin. Ralph took Hallelujah to shows in Kentucky, Ohio and Tennessee, where there were more professionally-trained pleasure horses and the competition was stiff. Horses in the plantation division are allowed to use a heavier shoe to enhance action; they went faster, had a bigger stride in back and higher animation in front. Some had a balanced look about them, but others squatted more on their rear ends and lifted their front legs higher than normal. Some were a little pacy, which gave more stride and speed, but that was not the correct Walking Horse gait.

Why did these horses look this way, and why did they usually win the top ribbons? I reviewed the history of the breed to find the answer. While reading Bob Womack's book, *The Echoes of Hoofbeats,* I could see what had happened to the Tennessee Walking Horse's development. It occurred because men wanted a fancier horse to show.

The show horses of the thirties and forties were ridden much more than today's show horses. They had stamina and their training demanded nothing out of the ordinary from them. The spectators liked speed, however, even though Tennessee Walking Horses were not developed for speed. When pushed beyond their natural ability, they started "breaking gait." They lost their four-beat smooth walking rhythm and began to pace and fling their hooves side to side or trot like a fancy Saddlebred. To get more speed in the gait, the horse would have to be trained for it. Trainers experimented and found that to have speed with the proper form, the horse needed to lift his knees higher. They put heavier shoes on his front feet, added some pads and made the horse tuck his chin more by holding the reins tighter and pushing the horse faster. The old timers insisted the Walking Horse was not designed for speed and doing so would ruin his natural gait. But the spectators approved of the horses' new way of moving and wanted more.

By the end of this era, the Tennessee Walking Horse was changed into a fancier mount, but he still performed his natural gaits at no discomfort to himself or his rider. There were no big secrets to his training. If one rode the horse at a farm, bought him and took him home, one could ride him the same as one did at the original farm. But trainers wondered if the horse could go even faster and do more if pushed further, so the training experimentation continued.

Ironically, the end of this era of the more natural training methods began in part because of an extraordinary bay gelding named Talk of the Town who came to the 1950 Celebration and won the Three Year Old Gelding Class. Talk of the Town wore nothing on his feet except a heavy shoe and he covered more ground than any other horse of that time. He had a most unusual rear leg movement, and he was able to drive his back feet up underneath and to the side of the front foot on the opposite side—a huge stride. He won the Celebration Grand Championship the next three years and in 1954, Mr. Sensation who had the same extraordinary movement won. This became the *new look*. It happened to be fairly natural to these two horses, but it would be copied by trainers using methods that were not natural and eventually became cause for embarrassment to much of the Tennessee Walking Horse world.

The desire for speed in the show horses caused more pacing blood to be added into the breed. It was found that a pacy colt could be "squared up" to move more like a trot with his front legs and could go faster with a more sweeping look to his rear legs. Because of this, mares who produced these pacier colts were in demand, and the colts out of these mares also were pacy. Speed and motion were what the show ring now demanded and in producing this, the wonderful, solid, natural, walking gait was slowly being bred out of the horses. Some horses not being developed for the show ring would continue to carry the old-time blood, but those would not bring the high prices that show horses brought, and it would take years for their value to become recognized again.

Because the new show horses were now pacier, something had to be done to get them to square up and walk with the bigger strides. In training, weight was added to the horse's front feet by using chains around the ankles. Talk of the Town had a big natural stride that needed only to be trained and controlled. Once he was trained, he kept his walk. He was a *Walking* Horse. Although Talk of the Town had kept walking when the chains were removed, most of the horses bred with pacing blood didn't react this way. They were pacing horses, and they went back to pacing when the chains weren't there. The Tennessee Walking Horse industry now had a big problem. They had developed a horse with a gait that couldn't be properly controlled at speed and most definitely couldn't be ridden for pleasure. I discovered this fact when I began breeding my own Tennessee Walkers.

Horses were trained with chains but weren't allowed to show with them. The next move was to allow show boots in the ring. This way the weight could continue to be on the horse as he was shown. Unfortunately, boots didn't have the same effect on the horse, who went back to pacing when the chains were replaced by the boots. The decision to legalize boots in 1955 wasn't met with approval by all horsemen and trainers. They predicted this measure could allow for abuses to the horses. How right and insightful they were.

The practice of "soring" the feet of the Tennessee Walking Horse might have come about accidentally. One story relates that a trainer had a horse with swollen ankles. Caustic balsam was applied to blister out the swelling, and the medicine was allowed to remain on the horse for some time. This procedure is still an accepted method for relieving some kinds of lameness. It causes the tendons to tighten and relieves soreness. That in itself is not a bad thing, but in this story, apparently the owner of the horse came by and wanted to see him ridden. He was told of the horse's situation but wanted to see him ridden anyway.

This points to a fact still true today—it's the owner of the horse who many times causes problems for the horses and trainers. The blue ribbon becomes more desired than the well being of the horse. Since that was the case, the horse was brought out and chains applied as usual. Because the blistering agent to treat the horse's legs caused pain when the chains hit them, he moved in a spectacular fashion, lifting his front legs much higher by throwing them out in front of his body and squatting back on his hind legs to help protect the hurting front ones as he gaited around the ring.

Whether this was the first soring done to a Tennessee Walking Horse or not, the technique soon began to see wide use.

A soring chemical such as kerosene or mustard oil was applied to the pastern or ankle of the horse. When rubbed by a boot or chain as the horse was ridden, it caused pain that made a pacy horse really "hit a lick." This was a new term, meaning to step high and far; the fans loved it and soon even the judges accepted this look as standard. This again points to a continuing problem with horse shows—what the fans like and the judges place becomes desired, regardless of what it does to the animal. Now there were a lot of horses that moved like Talk of the Town and Mr. Sensation, but they didn't come from selective breeding for a true honest walking gait—their accomplishments were artificial, from chemically-induced reactions.

In 1997, Don Bell was fired from his position as the Walking Horse Industry's Director of Judges after trying for four years to change the judging criteria. In 2000, he was interviewed by Andrew G. Lang, an ASPCA (American Society for the Protection of Cruelty to Animals) veterinarian. Bell stated that if the industry's own rules were followed, judges could "eliminate sore-looking horses that walk with a crampy gait." But the judges didn't and the exaggerated grotesque movements continued.

A problem with chemical training is you can't guarantee the results. One foot might react more to the procedure than another and the horse would be "off." Nature tried to help the horse by numbing the area so it no longer reacted as acutely to the chain. Thus the horses were sored in greater amounts so when some effects wore off, the horse would still perform. By causing sore areas on the ankles and not allowing or perhaps not wanting them to heal, the problem was made worse for the horse. Eventually the healing process caused ugly calluses and scars to form over this area. Many animals were scarred for life; some were even crippled.

Another dire aspect of the soring technique was that a great horse with natural ability, who could have performed admirably if given the proper old-fashioned training, couldn't handle this short-cut procedure and flunked out of the show strings and future gene pools. Other not-so-talented horses responded to this approach, became noted show horses and breeding stock, worsening the natural gene pool.

Not every trainer or owner was unmindful of his horse. Some didn't use this technique; others took such good care of the animals that they didn't suffer permanent scarring or harm. There were many, however, who were uncaring of the damage they were causing their horses.

In the early 1960s, outrage over sored horses helped to mobilize the equine welfare movement. Joan Blue, who was associated with a humane association, bought a horse at one of the horse sales that took place after the Celebration Horse Show. The horse's name was Pappa Charcoal, and the horrible condition of his front legs received national attention. Graphic photos of the horse appeared in national news magazines. In 1969, Senator Joseph Tydings (D-MD) introduced federal legislation for the protection of the treatment of the feral horses on public lands and against the prevalence of soring. In 1973, the same year our family moved to our new farm and began breeding horses, the Tennessee Walking Horse industry started an inspection program at horse shows to catch horses who had been sored and refuse them entry into the ring. Chain weight was also limited. These stewards were called a Designated Qualified Person or a DQP.

In my opinion, and that of numerous other naturally gaited, non-sored Walking Horse owners, this plan failed miserably. As reported in *Horse Illustrated,* in July 2004, recently retired USDA veterinarian, Tom James said he was convinced the system was so corrupt it had no excuse to exist at all. Sored horses were still allowed into the show ring. The DQPs were many times friends of the trainers and turned a blind eye. Intimidation played a part. Dr. Lang, an ASPCA veterinarian who followed and reported on soring issues, reported in the same *Horse Illustrated* issue that some USDA veterinarians who wrote a high number of violations, received death threats. According to the USDA's *Horse Protection Enforcement, Calendar Year 2000,* the USDA had to request that U.S. Marshals and law enforcement agents to accompany the inspectors to numerous shows.

The Horse Protection Act and consequent inspections did, however, put a stop to the *blatant* disregard for the well being of the animal. Open wounds and bleeding were absolutely forbidden. As time progressed, soring simply became a way of life. Some trainers were more judicious in its use; some seemed to have no idea that if a little was good, more definitely was not better. To many, training meant using a chemical and chain and having the horse stand in a stall with only limited riding.

At the present time, since open wounds of any kind are not allowed, inspection has become a process of palpation of the pastern area of the horse's leg to test for sensitivity caused by chemicals or misuse of the chains and improper after-care. Scars are not allowed. In fact, heated debate between government officials and the trainers over what is or is not a scar, caused a lot of turmoil within the industry. In 2007, a top government official stated that he attended horse shows filled with other high stepping horse breeds such as the Saddlebred and saw no scars or even calluses. Those horses also use chains in their training. Why didn't they have scars or calluses? The answer was obvious—they didn't use chemicals.

More sophisticated methods such as thermography which picked up heat emitted from inflamed areas on the ankles, were used to some advantage, but was costly and couldn't be used at every show. The bottom line was the industry had no real intention of totally cleaning up its act. They only wanted to change enough to slip through the inspection process. The abuse and soring issue had not been resolved.

"Fixing" was a new term that meant soring. The big lick or padded horses were shown on "built ups" or "stacks" usually made from leather or rubber pads which made their front feet longer and higher. Making these pads was rather specific for each horse because each animal had a slightly different way of moving. A specified ounce weight of chain about their pasterns was allowed in the show ring, and as heavy a chain as needed to accomplish "training" was used at home. Between the pads, chains and soring, the horse evolved far from his origin. Without realizing, considering or caring about the abuse the animal was given to achieve this look, the spectators approved.

In the early 1980s, when I started showing, the pleasure horses were for the most part ignored by the trainers. They were considered dull in the show rings, especially at the big Celebration in Shelbyville, Tennessee. While the pleasure horse classes were being exhibited, typically the spectators chose that time slot to get something to eat, saving their ring time to view more interesting big lick horses. The pleasure horses were left to the owners to show and to watch. Horse shows were mainly for the padded horses; only a few classes for pleasure horses were even included.

Pleasure horse people at the shows saw the padded horses standing in their stalls with all four feet "in a bucket." Instead of standing square on all four legs equally, in order to take the pain out of standing on their sored front legs, the horses shifted their weight back to their rear and put the front legs under their bellies. If there had been a big bucket under the horse, all four feet could have fit in it. When the horse stood like this overnight, he could hardly move the next day, and many times he would be whipped to get him moving out of the stall and keep walking.

I saw these things with my own eyes as I started showing my horses. I knew some big lick trainers who sored their show horses but definitely took better care of them. Not all trainers treated their horses with total disregard. Inspections by the DQPs did some good, but unscrupulous trainers did well circumventing the process, so eventually the USDA got into the act. They trained their own DQPs and when "The Government" appeared at a show, it was commonplace to see scores of horses loaded into their trailers and taken home. This had the industry saying the government was ruining their livelihood. However, those of us who showed sound horses always rejoiced to see the government inspectors arrive as it meant we would have a great show, do well with our sound horses and not be subjected to witnessing sored horses compete with us with their unnatural way of moving.

During this time while I was getting more involved with showing, getting more talented horses and learning how to ride them better, wouldn't you know it—the trainers decided the pleasure horse could possibly be made into a better show horse. Others as well as I wrote letters to the Tennessee Walking Horse publications stating that trainers getting involved with the pleasure horses would be a disaster for the horses. At this time most pleasure animals were a lot like the foundation horses; they were trail ridden at home, enjoyed as a family horse and then taken to some show events.

Some trainers were already training the pleasure Walker, but for the most part, they just rode the horses. There were no gimmicks to the training. Horses who paced or trotted were sent home. Because of what the industry had done with the breeding end of things, horses no longer were as natural in their gaits and were not all pleasurable. This posed a big problem for me as a budding breeder of Tennessee Walking Horses.

From the 1980s to the present, many changes have been made in the pleasure horse industry. Trainers became more involved. The pleasure horse was no longer looked upon as a dull show horse who when shown allowed folks time to leave and get something to eat. He slowly evolved into a flashy, big striding, knee-raised, pseudo big lick horse having little in common with the old plantation horse that had been ridden on Southern plantations up and down the rows of cotton and tobacco.

To accomplish this way of going, the pleasure horse was also sored. But there is a very large problem with soring a pleasure or plantation horse. He could not be shown with chains; thus the soring done to his legs would have to be harsher so that he would do a show lick without the benefit of chains. Therefore, more sophisticated methods were developed to produce pain. Pressure shoeing which involved putting tacks, screws or other objects between the shoe and the foot, exerted painful pressure on the foot, forcing the horse to snatch it off the ground quickly as he gaited. Welding a bead of metal to the underside of the shoe so it dug into the hoof at each step was another method. One shoe manufacturer of heavy plantation shoes made them higher on the inside than on the outside, causing uneven pressure and resulting in soreness. These methods couldn't be discerned without removing the shoe, for which there was no rule, or using thermography which was expensive and not commonplace. Therefore, these horses passed the palpation inspection and entered the show ring.

This then, was the arena into which I rode, starting out as an ignorant, innocent owner/exhibitor of Tennessee Walking Horses and becoming more and more heartbroken and disillusioned with what men were doing to my wonderful breed of choice. It is possible to train a Walking Horse to a certain degree of animation using natural training methods. To reach exaggerated animation requires artificial means. When both Sherri and Ralph competed with Hallelujah, they showed against many horses which had been sored, and they did very well. But as the years went by, it would be harder and harder to show sound horses against the sored ones. I found myself faced with a dilemma with no clear-cut answer.

More could be told of the continuing history of soring in the Walking Horse breed. It isn't my intention to do so, but rather give an overview so readers will understand how it affected my life and the lives of my horses. Whenever I told people I had Tennessee Walking Horses, without even taking a breath I quickly added, "But they are pleasure horses, and I *never* sore them."

CHAPTER NINETEEN
Accolades for Hallelujah

1991 had been a thrilling year as Hallelujah and Ralph blazed a wide path getting blues after blues. The negative element was seeing some of our competitors showing pleasure horses that were obviously sored. It was obvious because they moved in the customary fashion of squatting back on their rear legs more than was normal and with animation that was also beyond normal. The sad thing was that many of the horses thus trained and shown were winning first place. In my eyes they did not deserve it. Their gait was off, their heads were not shaking as a good Tennessee Walking Horse's should, and sometimes they even looked lame. How could they beat horses who were more balanced and proper?

The answer was again, as in old times, the judging. Most of the judges were big lick trainers. Some also trained pleasure horses, and they used the same technique they used on their big lick horses. They were used to seeing horses travel in this fashion. We have a saying that as a judge you tend to tie or place what you ride. You like a horse in the ring that reminds you of your own horses.

Not all of the judges looked at the plantation pleasure horse through these eyes. There were a handful of truly wonderful judges who remembered what a real plantation horse was supposed to look like. These were the ones who gave Hallelujah most of his blues over the other type of pleasure horse. We went to every show where these judges presided whenever we could. Even with this type of competition, Hallelujah completed the year by showing credibly at the Celebration in Tennessee–at least with Ralph riding him–and by being the Walking Horse Owner's Association

High Point Three-Year-Old. It had been an exciting year, but the shadow of soring these beautiful horses was dampening my pleasure. Why did winning the blue mean so much that pain was inflicted on purpose?

I brought Hallelujah home for the winter for some rest and recuperation time. It was sporting of Ralph to allow me to do this. Trainers like to keep the horses in training and in their control the whole year. Who knows what an owner might do to the horse when the trainer could not oversee. I was pleased with this opportunity. It would give me a chance to ride him during the winter and re-establish our connection as well as allow my horse some outdoor time.

After returning from the Celebration where I hadn't ridden my horse to my expectations, I did some serious soul searching. With time elapsed, I contemplated my downfall, and I realized several things. First of all, even though I got ninth place, we had still beaten ten horses. Not too shabby for a nervous first time competitor in the big oval ring. The mistake that occurred wasn't Hallelujah's fault; he only responded to my cues as he had been taught. I had blamed Ralph for pushing me past my comfort zone, but I could have turned a deaf ear and ridden the best I could. Ralph was only trying to encourage us do our best, so the whole thing wasn't a fault situation. I needed to chalk it up to live and learn.

Remembering the new and exciting times we had as a family while showing this spectacular horse with Ralph as his trainer, I decided that having a horse in training was something I wanted to continue. My goal was to have a high-performance pleasure horse—to show with the best of them— and win. To that end, I needed a trainer. After all, I didn't know how to train, ride or show this type of horse, so I decided to take my four-year-old stallion back to Ralph for another season. In early spring of 1992, we made the trip. Ralph was happy at the prospect; Hallelujah seemed less so. When I led him into the barn and started to lead him into the tie area, he balked. I had never seen him do this before–ever. With a little encouragement, he stepped in, but I was disturbed by his reticence.

We started the year with our customary winning style, but Hallelujah was having more problems with the pasterns of his front feet. Horse legs seem susceptible to all kinds of injuries and infections, but under normal circumstances the owner or trainer simply applies a topical salve while the injury or soreness heals. In Hallelujah's case, his pasterns had been a minor issue last year, but now it was worse. It was a worry to get him inspected by officials before he entered the show ring and afterwards if he won the blue. Horses that received first place, and sometimes second or even third, were re-inspected as they left the ring. The reason was a horse could be sored just before the show, given some topical anesthetic to deaden the pain so they could pass inspection, and then enter the ring and show. It could wear off by the time he left the ring and they would get caught by the inspectors.

Hallelujah's pastern condition eventually got bad enough Ralph wanted to send him to Purdue Veterinarian School to see what was wrong with him. Hallelujah didn't seem very happy that year, and I opted to bring him home instead. I never had any issue with his feet while he was home; I reasoned maybe he just needed a rest.

Some of my acquaintances suggested Ralph was soring my horse. I thought not because if that had been the case, Ralph would have known what to do—or not do—to heal him and would never have suggested we take the horse to Purdue. Ralph wanted to keep Hallelujah to show; I was certain he wouldn't have done anything to jeopardize that. I had my farm veterinarian look at his pasterns and he gave me a salve. Eventually, over the course of a month they healed, but it would be several years later before we discovered the cause of his problem—something so simple and avoidable.

Now I was on my own. I had a big-going, plantation show-horse stallion and what was I going to do with him? By now I had more education in showing this type of horse, but I didn't feel very confident in training him myself or dealing with a much more powerful stallion than little Xanadu had been. I had quite an investment in this horse, and I didn't want to see him turn into a trail horse, putzing around on the farm or going downhill in the show ring.

As soon as his feet healed, I started riding him again. He was still rather pumped up from being at Ralph's, so he had more spring to his step. He tried hard to work for me. I felt less than confident, but there was a small Michigan show coming up, and Michal and I decided to take just Hallelujah. We wanted to focus only on him; that would be enough of a challenge. Actually, we were either pretty stupid or pretty brave because this was a little show ring at a farm. Horses were tied to the parked trailers before they were shown. I was able to rent a stall in their barn for my stallion. I had no assurances that he would stand tied to a trailer all day. It was a very different situation from the shows where Ralph had taken him.

This was the first time I had been responsible for getting Hallelujah ready for a class. Ralph always lunged him on a long rope before his first class, allowing him to run and buck a little to get the explosive energy out before I rode. (A lunge line is a rope about 30 feet long attached to the horse's halter and the other end held in one's hand. Used as a training tool, the horse is directed out and away from the handler and goes around in a circle with one in the middle. The horse can walk, trot or canter as directed.) How would he react at a show in a field, lunging in the open with no fences around in case he got free from me? How much should I ride him before we entered our class? Would he behave himself around mares and geldings as I led him to the check-in area, and how would he react to being checked? To this day, I still remember the butterflies in my stomach as we prepared him for his first class. This was a really big deal. Would I fall flat on my face–literally, or just make a fool of myself?

I remember my fellow exhibitors and friends asking why he was not with Ralph and looking at me as if I had two noses or something. Why would I mess with a good thing? They understood my reasoning about his feet but took a wait and see attitude. That's what Michal and I were doing, too.

Surprisingly, things went very well. Hallelujah was on good behavior, and I got over my case of nerves as soon as I entered the ring for my first class. Sherri, his first trainer, was the judge–how odd was that? It was good in one way because she knew the horse but bad in another because she knew how good he could be and would I measure up? We won that class and the other we entered. I wasn't puffed up with ego, but I was euphoric. I felt lucky. I loved my wonderful stallion as never before. Michal and I rode home from the show in shock and awe. By golly, we had done it!

Okay, so it was a small show, and Sherri was the judge. She was fair and liked natural plantation horses, but it was still a great beginning. We made plans to go to the International in Murfreesboro, Tennessee. It was the second biggest and prestigious show in the country next to the Celebration, and it was only a month away. Whatever were we thinking?

CHAPTER TWENTY

On Our Own

The trip to Tennessee was five hundred miles one way from northern Indiana and would take nine to ten hours if there were no delays. I practiced and practiced with Hallelujah and we got better in tune with each other. He no longer intimidated me as much as before. On the appointed day, we loaded up: Hallelujah in the trailer, Michal behind the wheel, me as the navigator and Chessa the film maker with the video camera. In our sublime innocence, we headed down the road.

By the time we had definitely decided to go to the International, it was very close to the show date. Our stall ended up being outside underneath a tent because there were many entries and the better stalls were already taken. The show was approximately a week-long, but because of Michal's job and schedule as a police officer, we competed only the last three days.

Praise Hallelujah was a good boy. In the mornings we exercised him in the big show ring along with the other contestants. The actual classes were in the afternoons and evenings. The problem was having no good place to warm my horse up just before I entered the class, which was almost a necessity. My horse needed to get his muscles stretched and warmed, and he needed a little exercise to take off the edge. Once Hallelujah was inspected, I couldn't leave the small waiting area.

It was at this show in 1992, that we saw a lot of sored pleasure horses. The sored horses were not warmed up much, just enough that they would go forward. If they did too much warming up before the class, they wouldn't be able to keep it together to finish. It was sad. These horses had passed the inspection, but again I wondered—how?

I was always nervous before the classes, less so when I finally got on my horse, and the nervousness passed away when I entered the show ring. There was too much to do and think about to have butterflies then. Our class was called and we began filing into the arena. I wanted to make a good impression first off, so I pushed my horse to get in gear right away. Hallelujah heard the music and the yelling of the crowd, and he was more than ready to show off.

He and I did better without Ralph's high-powered grain and living in a stall all day. Of course, at the shows he had to be stalled all the time, but somehow he was not the keg of dynamite he had been the previous year. In our first class, we got a fifth-place ribbon—not bad at all for the level of competition and number of contestants. Not all the horses were trained with questionable methods. Many were horses we competed with at our more local shows that also went to the International, and we saw a lot of familiar faces. Fifth was good enough to avoid embarrassment.

In our next class, we got a third and a surprise. As I left the ring, an official motioned for me to come to him. I was confused and apprehensive. Had I done something wrong? Was there something wrong with Hallelujah? My heart skipped several beats as I complied. It turned out that all he wanted was to inspect my third place winner. He was "The Government." Of course, we passed inspection.

Our crowning achievement was winning the Amateur Three-Gait Reserve Championship—not the Grand Championship but just a regular class. That was good enough for us. Chessa got it all on tape for posterity. Her, "Way to go, Mom!" comment can easily be heard. Yeah, *way to go!*

We got encouragement from competitors and spectators alike. One in particular said that we had proved we did not need a trainer; Hallelujah had looked great. In truth, he didn't look as spectacular as when Ralph had him, and I knew it. He didn't have the action, and he was not balanced on his rear legs as well as he could be. All the same, we had done exceptionally well at a very prestigious show. I was pleased but not satisfied. I wanted him to look as he did when Ralph had shown him. I wanted us to be the very best we could be. We needed to be brilliant to compete with professionally trained (and perhaps sored) horses in the future. I wasn't sure how I would accomplish it, but I had faith.

We headed home with a new goal. As well as perfecting our showing talents, I would stand Praise Hallelujah at stud starting that November and continue to show him in the spring.

CHAPTER TWENTY-ONE

The Praise Dynasty Begins

S ince Praise Hallelujah wasn't the first stallion I used for breeding on my farm, I was not a novice and I knew that each is different. Delight's Headman by World Grand Champion Sun's Delight was a terror to breed. Supreme's Xanadu by World Grand Champion Threat's Supreme was almost too lackadaisical about the whole business. I found out later several of my competitor acquaintances and even some friends were betting that if I started breeding Hallelujah, I would never be able to show him again. This wouldn't be an uncommon situation for stallions whose new interest in mares after they've been bred becomes too distracting at shows. Most are not bred until after their exhibition days have ended. At one point while my stallion was in training with Ralph, he strongly suggested I have Hallelujah gelded. From my abrupt answer, Ralph quickly concluded that would never happen.

Hallelujah was never studdish to show, or when around other show animals and people, but he had a lot of energy, and he knew when it was time for a class. He didn't want to stand still; he wanted to walk around or stand shaking his head up and down continually. He could be a handful, but I saw this not as stallion behavior but as a horse that was full of himself and wanting to strut his stuff. At any rate, I wanted to breed him so he kept all his parts.

That November I bred him to Candledance, my best mare, because I felt she and Hallelujah would be a wonderful cross. Both walked to perfection. Candledance was a large mare with a quiet, loving disposition. She already had one fine colt by Xanadu. I wanted to have the very first baby from Hallelujah before other people bred their mares to him. The Walking Horse registry is a little different from other breeds. Any baby born after October first is considered to be next year's foal for showing purposes with all new foals regarded as one year of age on January first. A fall colt would be months older, but still considered a one-year-old. This was a plus if you had a show career planned for the foal.

We now had a large, new barn with many stalls and an inside riding area, but we still had our little barn across the driveway where I continued to use my old breeding area. Praise Hallelujah lived in the new barn and that necessitated leading him from there to the little barn, a distance of about two-hundred feet from his stall door to the mare. The first time he made the trip, he had no idea what awaited him or what was expected of him. Candledance was a big mare, but she had been bred before and was very cooperative. It's recommended by stud managers that you not breed virgin mares to virgin stallions. Someone should know what is expected.

Xanadu had figured the procedure out all by himself when I let him continue living in the pasture with a group of mares. He was only eighteen months old, and I'd been sure I would spot any amorous mares as soon as he did and remove them from his reach. They flummoxed me, however, and two became pregnant with no visible sign of the romance. Xanadu's education carried over into my supervised breeding situations. He was ever careful. If a mare so much as laid back an ear or cocked a hind leg, he was not interested. Delight didn't care about any preliminary niceties to the mare. I had two comments about Delight: he would probably breed the tractor if it was in his breeding spot, and he could be considered a horse rapist. Regardless of technique, he had produced some outstanding foals.

By comparison, Hallelujah was wonderful. He was not driven by hormones like Delight nor indifferent like Xanadu. He got the job done with little fanfare. It is important when breeding a stallion, especially one that you wish to continue riding and showing, to have "that special place." They equate the place with the action, and it cuts down on their thinking that they will breed a mare any time or place they find one. During a show some time later, I was asked to breed someone's mare at the show because "she is in heat and she is here and so is the stallion…" *No way.*

Something else I added to Hallelujah's breeding routine was his apple cigarette. My horses get apples or carrots after each ride, so why not one after something as important as breeding a mare? It worked well as a reward for a job well done and later helped me with a breeding problem. I also used it as a reward for walking calmly to the breeding spot. He got an apple before he was allowed to breed. It kept him focused on me without needing strong measures.

Gabriella and Hallelujah

The stud masters strongly recommended using a different halter or bridle for breeding, never the same piece of equipment one would use to ride. I used a stud chain fastened onto his halter in a certain fashion, and I never used it that way for anything else. It worked beautifully. As soon as he took one step out of his stall with the stud chain, he knew where he was going. He started calling to the mare, but was a gentleman with me, the apple-server.

Candledance was later checked in foal. I was delighted. I would be having the very first Hallelujah baby in the fall of 1993. The spring of 1993, we bred four outside mares and in the fall breeding period, three others. Compared with the many mares bred by Thoroughbred race horses, this was barely a drop in the bucket, but it was more than I'd ever bred during one season with either Delight or Xanadu. It was not bad for a small Indiana backyard breeder. Not only did we breed mares, but we also continued with our winning ways in the show ring throughout that year. We proved to our naysayers we could do both things at the same time.

The show season of 1993, was our first as Amateur Owned and Trained. In 1992, when I had taken Hallelujah home from Ralph, the trainer, I couldn't show him in this division. There was a required ninety-day period during which the horse was not professionally trained to qualify for this status. I knew when I showed at the 1992 International that Hallelujah and I were not the best that I wanted us to be. It was a grand start, but it was not enough.

A stroke of luck came from an unexpected source. Janet, one of my horse boarders, was taking riding lessons from an instructor in the South Bend area. He was a renowned three-day event instructor, teaching dressage, jumping and just good riding habits. Somehow she talked him into coming to my obscure barn in Goshen. I'd always loved dressage, and enjoyed reading about it and seeing the Lipizzaner horses perform their dressage routines. I tried to use the principles I read about in books to improve my riding skills, but it's really hard to read and then do it. Here was the chance of a lifetime to learn from an excellent instructor.

I discovered from reading that the basic principle in dressage is to teach the horse self carriage. Instead of plunking around with more of his weight on his front legs which is easy for the horse, he was taught through exercises and correct riding to shift his weight back onto his haunches and elevate his front. That was exactly what soring did to a Walking Horse, only with disastrous effects to the horse.

I knew if I was to be highly competitive in my field, I had to learn to make my horse perform like a sored horse but keep him healthy and happy. Learning dressage techniques just might be my ticket.

CHAPTER TWENTY-TWO

Dressage and Mr. Sherman

For me, Charles Sherman was unsurpassed in teaching dressage to Walking Horses. I've had riding coaches since and tried to recommend dressage instructors to other Walking Horse people, but they never worked out like Charles. Tennessee Walking Horses are different from trotting horses. They move differently and their conformation is different. When a horse trots, there is a moment of suspension when all four legs are off the ground at the same time. A Walker always has one leg on the ground as he moves forward. He is supposed to float forward, not move vertically in the process, as a trotting horse does, especially when pushed for more action.

Charles hadn't worked with Walking Horses other than Janet's pleasure trail Walker, but he quickly figured out what I needed in order to make Hallelujah a better show horse. It would be a lot like an extended trot but with animation–forward moving and showy. This is a hard concept to comprehend. Several of the dressage teachers I tried after Charles moved away actually told me they didn't know what to do with a horse that wouldn't trot.

The principal of dressage is self carriage. The horse must be strong and supple to do the dressage maneuvers. This takes much saddle time building the horse's muscles through forward movements such as the flat walk and running walk, but also in lateral movements, teaching the horse to go sideways and forward at the same time called leg yielding and half passing. These exercises make the rear of the horse strong and his back supple. I was endeavoring to teach Hallelujah to carry his weight more on his rear legs freeing up his shoulders. If he could do that, then he should be able to snap his front feet high and throw them forward in a pretty arc. He had the proper conformation to do this; some horses don't and could never make the kind of show horse I now wanted. Xanadu did not have it. He was a lovely and talented stallion, but his niche was in versatility. He had a super mind and a very pleasing trail-type gait; he jumped and worked trail obstacle classes, but he was not built like Hallelujah.

What a contrast this was going to be to the sored plantation show horse. Those poor animals stood in their stalls all day long. Since they were trained by soring, they couldn't be ridden very long at a time because it hurt too much. This is what the trainers wanted. They got action in the front and hind leg movement with very little work. In this manner a trainer could train many more horses than if he had to ride them each for at least half an hour each day. The horses were not conditioned, they were "made."

The old timers had yet another training method. One told his rider, "Take him out on the dirt roads and don't bring him back until he's walking." It might take a long time, but when the young horse settled down and was too tired to do much else, he'd most likely do the head shaking, ear flopping, four-beat flat walk that was desired. No short-cuts, just hard work. I had to make Hallelujah perform as desired without crippling him or exhausting both of us in the process. Besides, Hallelujah gaited just fine; I needed more action and panache.

The first day Charles came to the farm, I was nervous. Here was a well-known local trainer, and I was ignorant about what I needed to do. I'd read dressage books, but generally got more confused. The first thing Charles said when he saw Hallelujah endeared him to my heart forever, "What a beautiful animal!" Excellent, that was definitely starting off on the right foot, but what would he think of me as a rider, I wondered? I mounted Hallelujah and off we went to the outside arena. "You have to teach your horse to move off his back end," he said. "Don't worry about the front; it will take care of itself." Being more or less a novice, I figured we would start off making the horse lift his front legs higher. I thought he already had a good back end, as we say. What I needed was a fancy front.

I soon learned my legs were made for more that walking and sticking in the stirrups of my saddle. "Leg, leg, more leg!" Charles yelled, as he taught me to use my legs on Hallelujah's sides to push him over sideways while still moving forward. This was a "leg yield" and accomplished by using my right leg to push Hallelujah to the left and vice versa. This is where having longer legs would be beneficial. Mine were short. Charles told me to wear English-type spurs to help me, not the wicked looking kind Ralph had used. Another exercise he taught us was the shoulder in. The horse goes around the arena with his shoulder slightly to the inside, so he moves with his spine very slightly bent. This strengthened his hind legs and loosened up his back. "Leg, more leg!" or "*Push* him over." I heard those words in my sleep.

Next I learned to use my legs to push the horse up into the bridle. Again it was "leg, more leg." There are several ways to get the forward motion one needs. Ralph used big spurs. I never saw any misuse of them, but I am sure all his horses knew what they were for. He also fed the horse lots of high-powered grain. After being in a stall all day, stoked with energy food, his horses were more than ready to move forward when he rode them; this was their time to get out. That highly charged energy level had been too much for me to handle comfortably. I didn't feel in control at all. Some horses are born with a lot of spunky energy. That type needs to learn how to control it and use it for flash instead of speed. I never would have believed it if Ralph had told me this, but my stallion was actually a little on the lazy side or more kindly put, laid back. Unless, that is, he was performing the hated victory pass.

Charles told me that if I used my legs to push the horse forward, I would have more control, and it would be a steadier gait. I had to prod Hallelujah when I felt he was slowing down but before he actually slowed. I needed to be one step ahead of him all the time. Charles taught me to be a busy rider. He said, "No one should know what you are doing, but if you stopped doing it, your horse would show them." Later when Hallelujah and I became a team, I received comments like, "Wow, Hallelujah was brilliant tonight!" That was more than fine with me; my horse deserved it. If they only knew how hard I'd worked, they'd know we'd both been great!

Charles taught me exercises to strengthen Hallelujah's body, especially his back end. A horse's hocks are very important. Since he would be shifting his body weight back onto them, they needed to be strong. Charles had us turning around, keeping the horse's rear legs in place and only moving his front legs around, in a slow pivot. We walked forward, stopped, backed up several steps and then pushed off into a flat walk. Exercises such as these needed to be done in moderation.

One of my earlier horse friends had visited a dressage barn and came back with a brilliant idea to make her horse better. She used the backup then go forward routine. I observed her doing it over and over for her whole ride instead of using this technique just a little and then alternating it with riding forward around the arena for a time. On her next ride, her horse would not back up–period. A couple things had likely happened. His hind legs and back had become very sore, or he was simply totally turned off backing up. It was great to have Charles supervise us so that would not happen in my zealous ignorance. Hallelujah could not be made into a great performing horse in a few lessons; to hurry would be disastrous.

Another lesson was the half halt. I describe it as driving with the brakes every so often put on. In a halt or stop, you use your legs to push the horse up into a fixed hand on the reins instead of the rider's hands following the horse's movement as usual when riding forward. It is a pull back but very unobtrusive. The horse halts with his legs underneath him instead of behind him. It's a prettier, smoother and more balanced stop. Watching a beginning rider, one sees the stop made with a hard pull back on the reins. Much of the time the horse's nose goes up in the air, his back sinks lower and his legs stop in any old position. It is anything but appealing. Of course, the half halt must be taught to the horse. An uneducated horse would be confused as to why the rider was telling him to go and to stop at the same time.

The half halt doesn't stop the horse because it's used for just seconds and the rider ends it before the horse halts. It is used to balance the horse; it tells him to get his rear end under him more. Charles used it to teach Hallelujah to sit back on his rear more, and then when I drove him forward with my legs, he naturally elevated his front legs to a greater degree. Aha! Finally we were experiencing what I had hoped for–forward movement, balance, collection, and more leg lift all at the same time. All my sore leg muscles from those "leg, leg" commands were paying off. This all sounds fairly easy perhaps, but it took months for us to understand it, become strong enough to accomplish it and then many more months to perfect it.

Charles was a great teacher. He always rewarded us. Except to yell, "More leg," or "Half halt," he never raised his voice. At the end of the lesson he made us feel as though we had really accomplished something. Hallelujah liked him too. He always trained and worked better with Charles calling out instructions.

Several women usually took lessons when Charles came to the barn. Consequently we all were to be ready with our horses so there was no lag time between sessions. Hallelujah would stand or walk around quietly until it was our turn. Then he turned on the power; he would puff up and dance around a little, acting like the king he truly was. Charles would just laugh at him and say, "Okay, let's see what the big fellow has to show us today," and we were off to the arena.

CHAPTER TWENTY-THREE

The International

The International Show held in Murfreesboro, Tennessee, takes place just a few weeks before The Celebration. Many horses and people who go to the International stay until the Celebration. Hallelujah and I had already had a bad experience at the Celebration in 1991, when he broke into a canter when he was not supposed to, but aside from a still tender spot about that incident, some practical concerns weighed in when considering the Celebration. The entry fees were high and the judging was more likely to be political.

At most prestigious shows, many times it seemed to be who one knew rather than how good one's horse was. Trainers were judges and sometimes it was pretty obvious favors were given. The International, on the other hand, was more like the shows we had in Indiana and surrounding areas. The fees were lower and so was the payback if you won; but, it was more affordable.

Some of the very best flat-shod pleasure show horses in our local five-state showing area also went to the International. In addition, there were more horses we didn't know from western and southern states. Again, there were two divisions: amateur owned *and* trained, and the professionally-trained plantation horses ridden by their amateur owners.

I started lessons with Charles in the summer of 1993, and in the fall we decided we were ready for the 500-mile trip to Tennessee again. This time we also took two mares, a little chestnut named Amber and a big black mare we called Classy. Michal had also been taking lessons from Charles on Classy and Amber. Hallelujah was heavy shod meaning his front shoes weighed more. He would have more action because he worked against the weight. Classy and Amber were Lite Shod.

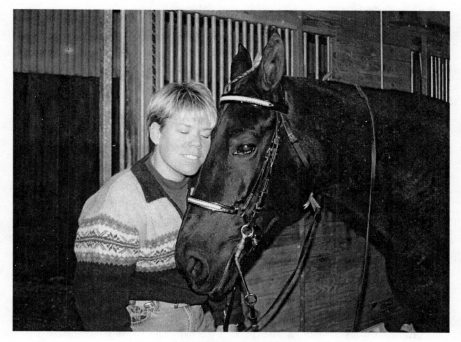

Michal and Classy

In 1986, I had served on the Tennessee Walking Horse Board of Directors as a representative from Indiana. I was pretty green around the edges about all the doings in the breed, but there was a push on to get some pleasure-oriented people on the board. This board made all the rules, and the pleasure folks who wanted to preserve the natural Walker wanted more input. The heavy-shod professionally trained plantation Walker was already showing, and those of us who didn't have one, or even understand the reason anyone would desire one, wanted to be sure there would be a division for those horses and owners who didn't compete with a heavy shoe. A rule must be made as to the exact measurement of the shoe size.

I was on the Pleasure Committee, and it was our task to come up with this dimension. We measured existing plain shoes at the nearby tack shop and came up with the size we thought would be right. It is the size still accepted today. Unfortunately, as the years went on from the 90s and into 2000, sly trainers found they could make the same size shoe but out of heavier metal and thus get an unfair edge. It was all about winning. In 1986, only the plantation horse with the heavier show shoes interested the trainers. The lite shod Walker was pretty much left to the amateurs for a few more years.

Classy was a hyper horse. When I bought her I didn't realize just how hyper, but she had good gaits and was a large, refined mare. I thought in the future she would mate well with Hallelujah so we tried to live with her nerves. She spooked a lot; in fact, she had a lot of trail dumps to her credit. The main problem was that she just had one speed—fast. This is not a good thing for either a trail horse or a show horse. Half halts used on Classy had the effect of the rider almost becoming airborne as she elevated her front end and almost sat on her behind.

When she was excited, she floated her front feet out in a hesitating movement. It was rather pretty, but it was not the proper gait for competition. She also could go so fast she "ran away from her hind legs." Instead of keeping them placed on the ground, one at a time, they would go too fast and she'd hop. Riding her was interesting to say the least. She didn't relax when we exercised her by letting her run around us on a lunge line either; it seemed to wind her up more or turn her into a soaking wet horse from nervous sweat. We finally got her under control by feeding her a magnesium horse supplement which is good for both human and horse nerves. On her it functioned as a natural calmer. She was still a handful, but she showed well and earned good ribbons.

Amber was a small, young, brown mare barely 15 hands high, but she was flashy. She had the correct shoulder conformation to make her front end come up very nicely. With Charles working with Michal, Amber was a horse to be reckoned with. Her back end was not as sweeping as Hallelujah's, but she was a cute package and the judges usually liked her. This was my dream team at the moment.

We felt more at home for our second trip to the International. I also made our stall reservations earlier and got more suitable stabling. Another really big difference was this year we could show our horses in the Amateur Owned and Trained Division. We would be showing on a more level playing field with others who trained their own horses.

It was a triumphal three days. Amber managed to get a reserve, or second place, in the Amateur Owned and Trained Lite Shod class, and Classy got several notable placings. Classy placed in nearly every class at any show where she was exhibited, but she seldom won the blue or even the reserve. That likely had something to do with her attitude. We said of her, "When she was good, she was very, very good, but when she was bad, she was *horrid.*" And, if she was going to be horrid, she would do it right in front of the judge so he would be sure to see her.

The big thrill, however, was Hallelujah. He was now a five-year-old stallion and could have made my life miserable, even dangerous, by calling to mares, not paying attention to my directions as I rode him, or just being too much horse for me to handle. I made sure to lunge him before I rode in order to work off at least some of that energy and to have Michal as a second person standing by for help if needed.

One morning before the classes began, we were lunging Hallelujah in the same arena that was used for the show. There were only two other people exercising their horses at that same time. The arena easily might have been much more occupied— thankfully it wasn't. Hallelujah was feeling frisky from a restful night in his stall after that 500-mile trip, so he was full of high jinks. Stallions love to smell hoping to find an amorous mare. He was trotting around at the end of his lunge line but had his nose to the ground, smelling where others had been.

Before I knew it, he'd put one front foot over the lunge line. Now there was no way I could control him; his leg was in the way, and I had to drop the rope. Michal had been watching and when she saw what happened, she quickly shut the gate that would have allowed him to escape and called to the other riders who happened to be close. We all envisioned a non-desirable, even dangerous, scenario: loose stallion attacks riders on their horses. That would have been just dreadful. The other riders left in a hurry, and I rushed up to get my horse. He had stopped and was just sniffing the ground, totally unconcerned about the other horses, as I quickly got him back on the line properly.

After that little incident, I always lunged him with side reins connected from his bit to a strap around his middle so he couldn't get his head down. Years later I had a chuckle after one of my fellow competitors asked me if lunging Hallelujah in that manner made him pick up his front feet higher. If she only knew.

The last night of our competition was to crown the Plantation Pleasure Amateur Grand Champion. I was more nervous for this class than the two previous regular classes that Praise Hallelujah had already won. This was for the big one. My friend Carolyn, who had been Hallelujah's masseuse for the show, did extra leg stretches and massaged his back. I felt my own muscles tighten and my stomach churn as I waited in the warm up area after inspection. This class would have professionally trained horses ridden by their amateur riders as well as those of us who trained our own animals.

Finally the gate call was heard, and we all headed for the opening into the arena. Riding a horse is not like riding a motorcycle. A horse has a mind of its own and exactly how it chooses to behave and perform, no one can predict. All the training may pay off or an embarrassing situation can unfold. Hallelujah was still canter happy. He loved that gait and would roll into it at the slightest provocation. I certainly didn't want a repeat of the Celebration. By holding my reins firmly and gently driving him with my legs, we made our entry. My stallion knew he was on parade and this was a special night. He performed the flat walk with slow measured cadence, never missing a beat with his head held high and nodding up and down, the trademark of a good Walking Horse.

The running walk was called and Hallelujah notched his speed up and floated around the ring. I always held my breath a little when I asked for the running walk as this was where he might decide to show the spectators and the judge his wonderful but unsolicited canter. Tonight he was picture perfect. The class was a canter class. Many Walking Horse classes do not use that third gait. I think this is so because a lot of riders cannot get their horses to canter and some horses seem either not to like it or cannot perform it well. To please the contestants and get more entries, the canter is often left out.

This Championship class would test all our abilities. As a team we performed admirably, but presumably, so had others. Standing in the line-up waiting for the judges' results, I dared hope we might be the winner. The wait seemed interminable as I smoothed my new dark teal riding coat bought just for this occasion and reminded myself to breathe. At last the results were called. "Number 500, Praise Hallelujah ridden by Rose Miller, Goshen, Indiana." And we were the Plantation Pleasure Amateur Grand Champion!

As the other placings were called and the ribbons handed out, Praise Hallelujah and I went to the winner's circle. Now I had a big decision to make. Would I be brave enough to make the victory pass? I could take a short-cut and leave the ring quickly. Hallelujah started dancing around a bit as the other horses left the ring. I walked him in a small circle to keep his energy from exploding until all the horses were gone. I decided to do it. How could I not? This was my first big win.

When the garland of yellow flowers was placed around my horse's neck, he got more agitated. Finally it was time to go. Turning him the long way around the arena I allowed him to go forward. I'd like to say it was a beautiful victory pass and the photograph taken was perfect, but it wasn't quite. Hallelujah had his head held too high, his nose stuck out too far and his feet were not in perfect rhythm, but we made it safely around and out the gate with the music playing and the crowd clapping. Michal met me as I exited the gate and held Hallelujah's reins while I dismounted. I was giddy from excitement. It had been a dream come true—me and my special horse, one I had trained myself, with an impressive victory at the International.

The International Horse Show was kind of a showcase of the way things were with the pleasure horses. The first two years we competed, two circumstances were in our favor. First was the judges. This big show was officiated by three judges placed at various points around the ring instead of a single judge as at smaller competitions. There was little room for error. If the horse made a mistake, it would likely be seen. Fortunately not every judge liked the new higher stepping look of the pleasure horse. These International judges leaned more to a natural going horse, giving us a very good chance of top ribbons.

The second was the trainers had not completely taken over the pleasure horse so their methods had not yet produced a horse with which no sound horse could compete. We reveled in our success.

In 1994, we again traveled to the International. This time two circumstances were against us. First was the judges, noted for liking the sored looking horse, and second was that Hallelujah was not quite himself. He was a little off as horsemen say. He wasn't limping lame nor was it obvious to an onlooker, but I knew. He didn't feel supple and fluid. He couldn't balance back and use his shoulders as he should. We traced it to his back; he had somehow sprained it, doing who knows what. Chiropractic horse treatment, acupuncture, massage and lots of liniment along with gentle riding were used. When the time came to leave, I debated with myself whether to go. We did–and I was about to learn a hard lesson.

I am sure the almost ten-hour trip in a horse trailer did nothing to help my stallion's back condition. I used the massage, liniment and muscle stretches, but he was still stiff. We got a fourth place in the Amateur Owned and Trained class, an eighth in the Amateur class and finally a tenth in another. I was crushed. Hallelujah never received such low placings. In order to protect his back, he sort of sunk it down which made his neck go up at a bad angle. His hind legs, instead of driving or pushing underneath his body, made shorter steps. All in all it was pretty ugly.

I had several fellow competitors ask me what was wrong with him as it was obvious he was not in his usual form. One woman asked me if I couldn't fix him. I explained that I was trying, using liniment, massages and so forth. After she left, Michal looked at me and said, "Mom, I don't think that is what she meant by 'fixing' him." We left for home the next day. We took some other horses that trip, but all I remember is how bad Hallelujah felt and looked.

The 1994 International Show had been a real bust, but something else occurred in that time frame that was a fascinating event. David Lichman, one of Pat Parelli's instructors, came to our New Acre Farm and put on a clinic. It was my first introduction into the "horse-whisper" type training. I knew David from my early International shows where he was a top competitor and frequent champion. The fact that he gave this country gal from Indiana some of his time and was nice to me at a strange and prestigious show made me cherish our acquaintance. When he came to my barn for the clinic, I was having some problems with my big stallion.

Praise Hallelujah had decided he didn't want to load into the trailer. He'd always been slow about it, sniffing manure left by other horses before he jumped in, but next he just stopped getting in. I really needed a horse whisperer. As David helped me through the clinic routine, one comment made me smile. "Boy," he said. "I got here just in time."

After spending some "one on one" time with Hallelujah, my horse decided getting into the trailer was no big deal at all. Throughout the rest of his life all I had to do was open the door and point.

It had been rather obvious Hallelujah had the upper hand and was pushing me around. With David's expert help, we soon got our act together. At the end of the clinic, all the riders rode their animals with just one rope attached to a rope halter—no bridle or bit. I was afraid to try it on my stallion, but David assured me we could do it. And do it we did, much to my amazement and empowerment!

CHAPTER TWENTY-FOUR

The Breeding Shed

The 1994 International had been a bust, but we did extremely well otherwise in show ring competition. Hallelujah had an indisputable reputation and in 1993, had bred eight mares. Again, I must mention that I was breeding a specific horse, the Tennessee Walking Horse, that was not as popular as the Thoroughbred, Arabian, Quarter Horse or Standardbred race horses. My farm was not in middle Tennessee; it was in northern Indiana. Eight mares successfully in foal might not seem earth-shattering to anyone else in the business, but it was impressive enough to me.

I decided that in order to better use my stallion, I needed to get some breeding equipment that allowed me to collect his semen and either ship it in special containers to faraway mare owners or use artificial insemination to breed several at one time here on the farm. It was interesting about mares coming to the farm to be bred. No matter when they had been in heat the last time at home, once at my farm, they all synchronized their cycles in a short period so all the mares needed to be bred during the same week. If only they would plan it better and space their times over a longer period! This can be accomplished by using hormone injections as done at larger farms, but I hated to meddle with Mother Nature too much.

Hallelujah could not go on indefinitely breeding mares every day or even every other day. In the big Tennessee Walking Horse breeding barns, the stallions are collected three times per week, and you must accommodate that schedule by having your mare in estrus at the proper time. I didn't have that many mares to breed, but when they were all ready at the same time, it was too many. I could solve the problem if I could collect from him and breed more at one time. Most important was the breeding mount for the stallion to get on as he would a mare.

I studied stallion collection for some weeks before I decided what I wanted. I watched a local Arabian horse farm collect off a "dummy" mount, but someone had to hold the container called the artificial vagina or AV. Those stallions hit the AV with force, and I knew there was no way I could do that; I'd be knocked down for sure. Plus, a real mare held by another person on the other side of the dummy to encourage the stallion to jump on it was also present.

I wanted to be able to do this all by myself and still live to tell about it, so that was not for me. Another way collection was done was to use a real mare in heat and when the stallion mounted her, his parts were deflected into the AV which was held by a second person. This was the most dangerous way for all involved. It was the way my veterinarian had collected Hallelujah the first time to check his semen and be sure it was suitable for shipping—most definitely not a method for me.

Eventually I found a breeding mount that had the AV within it, and one obstacle was overcome. After the semen was collected, it had to be diluted with an extender made out of milk products and an antibiotic and kept at body temperature, so the sperm had nourishment as they were shipped. That meant I also needed an incubator to keep the extenders and all my mixing equipment at body temperature. A sperm counter, which would tell me how much extender I needed to add, a microscope to look at the sperm, and special shipping containers which kept the sperm at necessary temperature rounded out my needs.

Hal set the mount in concrete at the back end of the breeding wing of the new barn addition. I desired a place out of the way, yet inside, where I could use it in any weather. Many times I'd had to breed a mare outside the little barn with snow or rain falling. This time I wanted the best possible circumstances for my breeding enterprise.

After I had all my equipment set up and the mount was ready, the next hurdle was how do you teach a horse to breed a big black barrel with a hole in the end of it? I talked to lots of people; no one had a definitive answer, but everyone agreed a mare in heat should be involved. I had Hal build a narrow stall almost at a right angle to the mount. He put a back gate on it so my stallion couldn't get to the mare. The idea was for the mare to get the stallion excited enough so when he wanted to mount her, he wouldn't notice he was making love to a barrel instead of a live mare. Hallelujah could sniff her and even get his nose through the stall spaces, but he couldn't get his head in nor could he go over the top of the stall.

Believe it or not, it almost worked. Hallelujah nuzzled and nickered to the mare, and when he was ready, I pulled him over to the mount. Up he went, put the correct part in the hole, and then–nothing. The look he gave me was priceless. "What the heck was *that*?" he seemed to say. I held my breath and willed him to stay on the dummy and perform, but once it was clear nothing else would transpire and he slid back onto the ground, I gave him an apple and put him away. That was good enough for a first try.

We kept working on the procedure and after several weeks, he did what he was supposed to do. It took some time to figure out what temperature he wanted the AV to be and how much hot water to put in to control the tightness. His first success was cause for great cheering and many apples. Pretty soon he didn't need to have the mare be in heat just a warm body was good enough. This was a good thing because there wasn't always a mare in estrus when I needed to collect him. All was not roses, however.

The plan was for mare owners to call the day before they need to breed their mare telling me they want semen the next day. Then the pressure was on. It has to be collected, processed and shipped overnight by the last Fed Ex or UPS pickup time. Sometimes I had just live covered a mare or collected him for my farm's needs; either way, it would be a challenge to collect more semen that day. Every now and then Hallelujah would decide he just was not in the mood. If he didn't want to do it, he pretty much had control of the ball game.

I had several tricks I'd try. I started collecting in the mornings to give me more time if he wouldn't cooperate. I'd change mares in his tease stall. Sometimes another mare of a different color would perk him up. I tried herbal products with some success and lots of different vitamin supplements. There was only one time that we failed totally, and I had to call and apologize. I felt quite chagrined. Twice the shipments got lost in transit which was disappointing for all involved. It was too late to try again for the mare's heat cycle.

At a horse show during a lunch break, I saw a fellow show exhibitor who was a veterinarian and horse breeder. Dr. Charlene Cook had given me great support in getting started with stallion collection. She was in charge of several top-name Tennessee Walking Horse stallions at her clinic in

Georgia. At lunch I was complaining about how hard it was at times to get the job done. Charlene laughed and said, "I know, I hear the gals who collect our stallions talking and sometimes they get so mad at the studs." Well, that was an eye opener for me. Here I thought I was the only one who had that problem!

I carried on the apple-cigarette tradition in teaching and rewarding my horse for doing his job. And believe it or not during peak breeding season, it did seem like a job. Sometimes without much imagination I thought I heard him say, "Oh, darn, not that again!" or, "Don't bother me, I'm eating." Apples helped. Even if he tried to collect and didn't quite make it, he'd look at me for his apple which he always got. After all, he was frustrated and at times angry, getting off the mount with an irate squeal and sometimes a kick.

Breeding live mares was a different sort of challenge. I spent a lot of money and saw my veterinarian frequently for mare palpations. By rectally examining a mare, he could tell me the size of the ovarian follicle and how ripe or ready it was. This was important because I tried to utilize my stallion for only two live covers per mare. If the stallion isn't busy with numerous mares, the breeder can simply breed the mare every other day until she goes out of heat which is usually five to seven days and says, "No!"

Hallelujah learned to be cagey with his consorts as some of them worried both him and me. They were teasers, leading both of us to think they were really ready to mate, but when Hallelujah started to mount them, they could move back and forth or worse, kick. Sometimes he pushed his chest into their sides to test them out, nuzzling their necks and nickering stallion noises.

If he thought they were receptive, he danced around to the rear and did his job. My job was to be sure they were ready for his advances; but sometimes we both were fooled, and I put the mare away to try again the next day. Many large farms have a teaser stallion who checks out the mares but never breeds them. Hallelujah had to test his own, a job he really relished. This action according to documented facts, kept his testosterone at its highest level. Teasing, talking to and seeing the mares was better for his libido than actually servicing them.

Many breeders restrain the mares in one way or another while they are being bred. Perhaps because I am a woman, that went against my grain. If she wasn't in the mood, I tried to find out why and what could be done in place of forcing the mare to accept my stud's advances.

In the beginning, I used hobbles on the mares. They prevented the mares from kicking the stallion in his sensitive parts, but accidents still could occur. Occasionally when the stud came off the mare— more slowly and relaxed than he mounted them, his dangling front foot slipped into the rope of the hobble strap. Having the foresight to imagine a great catastrophe, I added panic snaps to the rings that I could pull quickly and release the hobble. Still it was a danger I decided I would live without. If the mare wasn't ready, I wouldn't tie her down. More teasing with stallion nuzzling and nickering usually did the trick. Some mares wanted to know their mates and they relaxed when he was stalled next to them for a day. Maiden or virgin mares were the worst. They could be quite prudish and want nothing to do with a rearing stallion at their hindquarters. Breeding mares with foals by their sides was another big challenge. How to take the mare from her foal and convince her to mate again was a dilemma. Some wanted to see the foal; others were convinced that the stallion would harm their babies.

Pasture breeding as Xanadu had done in his youth was certainly the best for the mare as the stud had to take his time and whisper lots of sweet nothings. It had a high conception rate too, but it was not possible when breeding diverse and numerous mares. Stud managers who use this method gather the all the mares to be serviced and turn in the stallion. No more mares can be added safely after that point as fighting would occur within the mare ranks. It was a closed sorority. Occasionally I wished I could turn Hallelujah in the pasture with a hard to settle mare, but that was impossible. He was used to his mares being tied up and ready to breed and I didn't want him injured.

I'm not sure that Delight's Headman, whom I'd owned in the 80s, would ever have been disinterested in breeding no matter how many mares were offered. He probably would have loved the phantom mare too, but he was somewhat of a danger to breed. Hallelujah was wonderfully gentle with both the mares and the handler. Perhaps his libido was somewhat less at times, but it worked great for breeding and showing at the same time. I didn't want a breeding machine; I wanted an all-around great horse, and he was that.

While standing Hallelujah at stud, I bought another stallion. This one was a different bloodline and would cross well with Hallelujah's daughters and mares of different breeding. Unfortunately, he was a terror to breed. He was gentle to handle and ride, so it took me completely by surprise that he

went bonkers when he saw a mare in the breeding area. The first time I tried breeding him he dragged me the last twenty feet, but I managed to keep holding his rope. He jumped sideways upon the poor mare who fortunately was one of mine not a customer's, and I could hardly pull him off. When I did get him back on the ground, he wheeled around and kicked her. He was *mad*! Somehow I managed to get him back to his stall and realized I needed reinforcements.

I called Eli, a young man with Amish background who is a natural horse whisperer. He'd worked with another young horse sired by Hallelujah I had rescued who was near crazed from mistreatment. He'd done wonders for that one; I hoped with all my heart he could fix this problem for me, too. Eli came, assessed the problem, and after some work was able to get the stallion to walk more quietly to the mare area, but the stud still went crazy when he got close to the mare, rearing and pulling Eli along with him. We didn't breed a mare that day; we were just trying to get the stallion more under control.

When my mare came back into season, Eli came to the barn and handled the stud. The horse was still nuts, but this time he managed to get on the right end of the mare and did his job. When he came down, he wheeled around and tried to kick her again, but Eli was too fast for him and got him off target. Next he reared and pawed the air above our heads. Darn, this wasn't good at all.

Amazingly, over time, this stallion finally got more controllable, and I bred him myself to several mares. The apple trick worked again but only after the fact. Even if offered an apple on the way to the breeding stall, he wouldn't stop his headlong rush to the mare, but as soon as he was done with his job, I pulled his head to me and offered him the apple. At that point it distracted—and interested him—enough that he stopped trying to kick the mare and paw the air, but he was never enjoyable to breed and eventually I gelded him. He made a wonderful riding horse. His libido had been too strong. I wouldn't trade Hallelujah's sometimes fed-up-to-here attitude about mares for one that would breed more mares but be less agreeable to manage. Hallelujah suited me just fine.

But I had more to learn regarding my stallion and his ideas about being the master of New Acre Farm.

CHAPTER TWENTY-FIVE

If the Saddle Fits

After the disastrous 1994 trip to the International in Tennessee, I worked hard to get Hallelujah back in shape. Eventually he returned to his previous abilities. One day in early winter, I was riding him in the inside arena when I noticed my saddle was making strange, squeaky noises. Nothing dire seemed to be happening so I kept using it, and I became aware that Hallelujah was working differently, in a superb way. It felt unusual and I didn't know precisely what he was doing. I asked a friend who happened to be there that day to video tape him so I could see what I felt in the saddle.

What I observed was a spectacular moving horse—and he was mine! He was striding up underneath himself in a wonderful way, but it was his front end that took my breath away. He was lifting his knees high, breaking level as we say—meaning his upper foreleg became parallel with the ground. A sound horse can hardly do more. As the soring of pleasure horses advanced, they would begin lifting their legs above level. Instead of just lifting his front legs up and then putting them down, he was "rolling out of his shoulder" throwing his front legs out in a beautiful arc. Goodness, how did this suddenly occur?

When Charles came for another lesson, he watched us, checked the saddle and came to the conclusion that the saddle tree had broken. That was the squeaking I was hearing. The saddle was under a warranty, so I sent it back and eventually received another one.

A saddle, at first glance, is just something to sit on and keep the rider on the horse. What most people don't realize is the *horse's* comfort must be paramount. The main part of a saddle is the frame or saddle tree which is made in different lengths and widths, usually out of resin bonded plywood laminates. Padding is added to the bottom for the comfort of the horse's back and some on the top for the rider; then it is covered with leather. While the old saddle was being replaced, which took a month, I tried all the other saddles in the barn on Hallelujah, hoping to recapture his marvelous way of moving. I couldn't. Heretofore, I had never really given my saddles any thought. If it fit me, it was a good saddle. To show the Walking Horses we used English-type saddles called cutbacks. They are larger than a racing saddle and smaller than a big Western saddle. They're designed to give the English going horse such as the Morgan, Arabian, Saddlebred and Tennessee Walking Horse more freedom for his shoulders so he can move them and lift his knees as high as possible. Western horses such as the Quarter Horse used the bigger saddles for roping and work around cattle.

Since I didn't have anything that allowed Hallelujah to move as before, I was frustrated. I contacted a saddle fitter and she came out to the barn with an electronic monitoring device she put under a saddle. When I sat on the saddle, we saw red spots appear on her television-like screen where the saddle pinched my horse's back. June and I came to the conclusion that Hallelujah had very wide shoulders and the reason he moved so wonderfully when the saddle tree broke was because it allowed his shoulders to roll really forward. The narrower saddle tree stopped him before he had reached his full stride. The broken one spread open with each stride.

Okay, now that I knew the problem, how could I fix it? June sent instructions and measurements to England for a special saddle to be custom made for Hallelujah. While waiting, I rode him in a wider Western saddle, which was the best I could do to accommodate his hefty shoulders. When the replacement for my broken saddle arrived, I could hardly wait to try it out. It didn't work! I still couldn't get that wonderful free movement of his shoulders. Eventually the saddle from England arrived and June brought it out. We tried it on and *it* didn't work! We were both flummoxed. This saddle supposedly had been made to the horse's exact measurements and designed by June specifically for a Walking Horse. What had gone wrong? Months later, after many calls to the saddle maker, she told me they admitted they had not made the saddle on a wide tree as requested; they had used a medium tree. It was like dangling a beautiful jewel at arm's length. No matter what I did I couldn't reach it.

At least now I knew my horse needed a wide saddle tree with a design that allowed his shoulder blades to move back far enough for a big stride forward before they hit the saddle. My original saddle, the replacement of the one that broke, was a comfortable saddle for both horse and rider. It worked on the other horses, but it needed to be wider for Hallelujah. I finally solved the dilemma by finding someone in my area who could spread the tree on that saddle. It was a very reasonably priced saddle, and I quickly bought several of them. They remain my favorite saddles to this day and each horse has his own size. Saddles are like shoes – they *must* fit the *horse*!

CHAPTER TWENTY-SIX

Successes and Change

After getting Hallelujah comfortably saddled, we continued our lessons and training with Charles. Hallelujah was performing very well, better than before the saddle episode. He was freer in the front and was throwing his front legs out nicely. He still didn't look as magnificent as he had with the broken saddle, but we had improved from before and that would have to be reward enough. So far we were undefeated in Amateur Owned and Trained classes in the five states where we competed.

Going to the International was becoming a habit, so at the end of August we packed up again. This time we took Hallelujah and Classy. Of the three judges chosen for the show, I knew two from past experience and I had faith in them to pick the natural horse versus the sored, crampy-moving animals. I didn't know the third judge at all. It could make a big difference in how we were placed in the classes.

As the years had gone on, the sored plantation horses which showed with Hallelujah were looking worse. As mentioned earlier, soring is not an exact science. Too much caustic substance on one foot made the horse look off or lame. Too much applied to the front feet and he could hardly pick them up or when he did they stomped back to the ground as if he had on cement boots. The trainers were trying to get more action in front and more stride behind, but it was obvious to even an untrained eye that some horses looked labored. The total picture wasn't pretty. Still, that was what some judges wanted.

The first day we showed Classy in two Western classes and she tied reserve in both. This was very good for her. Classy was lite shod and could be shown more frequently during the day. She didn't have to work as hard doing her gait as heavy-shod Hallelujah did. It was a gait like one would ride on a trail but fancier. I was careful of the number of classes I entered Hallelujah in because he worked very hard strutting his stuff. Then too, I wanted the spectators to look forward to seeing him and not saying, "Here comes that darn horse again," in a derogatory manner. He almost always won his classes and showing him in too many wouldn't endear me to my fellow competitors.

The next day it was time for Hallelujah, and he won an Amateur class. Later that evening, he won the Amateur Owned and Trained class unanimously. All three judges had him first on their cards instead of using a scoring system. The following day he won another Amateur class, this time requiring the canter. We had three blues already and a couple days to go. We were excited. Classy was good in her division–not a winner but pulling in decent ribbons of seconds through fifths. She earned her way.

Before entering the last Amateur class, Hallelujah was inspected by the DQP who happened to be a man we knew because he checked some of the northern shows. "Are you planning on showing him anymore?" he asked.

I replied, "Yes, tonight and tomorrow, too."

He showed me Hallelujah's left front pastern area and pointed out that his skin was pink under his one white foot. The DQP said he would pass for this class, but I had better not show him again because that area was probably going to become sensitive if I didn't do something about it. How was that for a situation? I was known for showing sound horses and when advertising Hallelujah at stud I always mentioned he was trained and shown sound. How embarrassing it would be to be turned down and written up. I'd paid no attention to his feet; I knew I didn't sore him, so he should be just fine. Another lesson learned—always check your horse's legs before inspection. He could have stepped on himself and caused a cut with blood—sure to get you in trouble. Innocence is not bliss.

I spent the next morning inquiring how to heal an honestly sore horse's pastern and got lots of advice; after all, there were many experts in *that* department. I was given some special salve and told to put it on Hallelujah, wrap the leg with Saran Wrap and then use my regular leg bandages. The use of the Saran Wrap was to sweat the salve into the sore area. This same wrap was also used extensively to drive caustic soring chemicals into the legs by trainers. How absolutely awkward it would be if any of my fellow, sound-horse competitors saw my horse standing in his stall with any plastic wrap–even cotton wraps on his legs–a sign of soring. Some already believed that I did something to him because he was so competitive even with sored horses. At one horse show closer to home, my friend Pat was standing along the show arena watching Hallelujah and me compete. A man eased over to her and asked, "What does Rose do to that horse?"

Pat assured him that I just rode him. He looked at her skeptically and answered, "Well, whatever it is, it isn't quite enough," and walked off. His comment verified that a totally sound show horse could be spectacular, but there was a definite difference in the look of sound versus sored—and totally sound just wasn't quite enough, if as a judge, owner or spectator you wanted a lot of action, correct or not.

Photo by David Pruett

Later in the day I talked to the DQP who knew I didn't sore my horse, and asked him what he thought had happened. His answer was an eye opener. He told me the arena footing was a mixture of very, very fine limestone dust and dirt. The grit of the fine limestone got flicked up into the pastern area and as the horse worked, the sand ground into his skin. Some horses were more sensitive; indeed, Classy had no problems. He suggested hosing off the horse's feet each time I worked or showed in any arena with this type footing.

When I got home, I laughingly told Ralph about my experience. He thought for a moment and then said, "I'll bet that is what happened to Hallelujah when I had him in training and we were having so many problems with his feet. I had just put in a new limestone riding area!" Since Ralph rode the horse every day but Sunday in that arena, it was no wonder his feet wouldn't heal. No matter what the trainer did to treat them, they kept getting re-irritated.

Perhaps there is a plan for our lives. Perhaps I was meant to train, show and care for my stallion on my own. I don't know how it would have turned out if Hallelujah hadn't gotten sore legs while with Ralph. I'm sure I would have left him longer. Although it was frightening in the beginning, traveling down the road to success without a trainer was very rewarding and fulfilling. How very different my life and career might have been if Ralph hadn't put in that newly graveled arena!

Hallelujah healed and was ready for the Championship classes, having rested one full day in his wraps. He won the Amateur Owned and Trained Grand Championship, and we had clinched our second International Grand Championship! That week I got numerous favorable comments from friends on Hallelujah's way of going. Even one of the judges remarked to me she had never seen him better, thanks to Charles Sherman, a broken saddle and lots of hard work. Classy did her best too, pulling in a Reserve Lite Shod Grand Championship. We came home in great spirits.

That year brought about a big change in my horse herd. I was on Cloud Nine with our successes, but it took a lot of work keeping top show animals in prime condition and riding for fun on Xanadu had taken a back seat. I still loved him dearly, but time constraints caused my little black stallion to spend more time without me. I'd gone from riding him twice a day many days to not riding him for weeks.

Among my horse boarders was a lady who had an Arabian horse she didn't enjoy riding. I let her ride Xanadu, her first experience with a Walker. She was hooked much as I had been with my first ride. We made an agreement; she would purchase him, geld him and board him on the farm.

Xanadu was now fifteen years old and took his gelding in stride. His new owner had lots of time for grooming and riding. She enjoyed his safe gentleness the same as I had. After the winter months had passed, and the pastures turned green with luscious grass, we turned him out with all the rest of the horses and held our breath. What would happen? Would he enjoy his new freedom or dash around reminding all of them who he had been and maybe still thought he was?

We decided to put him in the mixed herd with both geldings and mares. He galloped out with his tail up, his mane flying and ears pricked forward. He stopped at a mare, whispered some sweet nothings in her ear, she squealed and told him to "buzz off." He went on to another. After he'd touched noses or flanks with most of the horses, he turned his attention to the thick grass of the pasture. He dropped his head and began to graze. His stallion paddock was not a pasture, and eating grass had always been a big treat.

It was as though he was fully retired now and free to enjoy life with his new friends and eat and eat and eat. No more did he need worry about what another horse was doing or where it was. Xanadu approved of his new life.

He was twenty-four when he passed away under a tree, having lived a most fulfilled life.

CHAPTER TWENTY-SEVEN

Black Cashmier and Final Praise

When we went to the 1993 International, Michal and I also went horse shopping. I was breeding mares which belonged to other people, but I didn't have a high-quality mare of my own to mate with Hallelujah. Each time I'd bred him to my great mare, Candledance, she'd produced twins with the typical results of having none survive. We went to one of the big breeding barns, and I asked the owner to show me some yearling fillies. I had a certain type in mind and her stallion, Pride's Final Edition, produced that kind. She showed me several and I shook my head. Those were not what I wanted. She finally said, "I think I know what you are looking for," and told one of the boys to get "Sarah."

Out of the barn came someone leading a stunning black filly. She was on the small side, but she had that natural swagger—that "loose" movement I was looking for. I guess I intuitively knew Hallelujah would cross best with that kind of mare. My, but she was a fine piece of horseflesh! I had to stop myself from drooling. With my heart in my mouth, I asked the price and cringed as I waited to hear the answer. The price she told me almost made me gasp, not because it was so high, but because it actually was in my price range. Without a moment's hesitation, I said, "I'll take her!"

There was no, "Well, I'll have to think about it and let you know tomorrow." It was a good thing too, because she wouldn't have been for sale the next day. When her husband heard she was selling Sarah and the price agreed upon, he was none too happy. I still distinctly remember the look of disgust on his face. He said he'd wanted to show her as a yearling at the Celebration and wondered if I would bring her back to put in training with him when she was two years old. I thanked him, but declined. Sarah was staying in Indiana.

They delivered her to the International show grounds and we loaded her up for the trip home. She was a little spitfire. Michal had lunged her in one of the show arenas for exercise before we put her in the trailer and could barely keep hold of the rope. Sarah plunged around, reared and bucked, and people watching shook their heads. They knew I'd been looking for a mare and I thought they'd admire this stunning young horse. But from their reactions I had to wonder what they knew about my new purchase I didn't.

We made it home in fine shape and began training Sarah who I renamed Final's Black Cashmier. She was ornery and stubborn, but I think a lot of it was because she really hadn't been handled enough. In fact, she'd been exhibited at the Celebration as a weanling, but the method was to take the six-month-old or even younger babies, teach them to lead and pose for a few weeks before the show, and then turn them out in the pasture again— no continuity of training at all. Instead I took lots of time and patience with her and it paid off. Cashmier became a gentle mare.

Two years later when she was three, I mated her with Hallelujah, and eleven months afterward while we were at a horse show, she had her foal. Bob, who did chores for me when we were gone, went out to do morning feeding and there was a very little, black foal in her stall. He called me, and I had many questions, none of which he could answer except that it seemed healthy and was nursing. He didn't know if it was a boy or girl. I was so excited; finally I had a Praise Hallelujah baby. We left the show early to come home and see it. It was a stud colt, and I named him Final Praise after both his parents.

He was a sweet foal, and he had exactly the walk I wanted. It was a cross between his mother's swagger and Hallelujah's power walk. I was enthralled with my new baby. Here was my new show horse. Michal and I began teaching him to lead. It's typically reasonably easy: one leads the mother, and the baby follows along beside her with a small halter on his little head with the lead rope held by another person. The foal should just go along quietly and happily, maybe running around a little, but learning he can go only so far before the rope stops him. Well, not Final Praise; he had a mind of his own. When we tried to put the halter on him, he tossed his head all around making even that a challenge. The leading of the little fellow got no better. I'd never had one put up such a fight at such an early age. It was as though his mind just switched off. You couldn't coax or prod him. He was like the proverbial mule. And then I remembered something...

When I was about twelve years old, my parents had been given a book entitled *The Work of Invisible Helpers*, by Amber M. Tuttle written in 1945. It was a mystical book, written to tell stories about special people on the earth who could leave their earthly bodies during sleep and go about the world helping people and animals. Today many believe in this mystical, psychic phenomenon, so you may or may not believe this is possible, but I knew at that young age I wanted to be an Invisible Helper. I would, of course, specialize in helping the animals. My mother was not at all supportive of my idea telling me that I needed to concentrate on being a *visible* helper first. I never became an Invisible Helper, but I always dreamed of being able to talk to animals. I couldn't do it, but I knew about a woman who could—and she could do it over the telephone. I hurried to find her number and make an appointment so I could talk to this little horse who was getting the better of me.

I called Mary Long and it was the beginning of many years of friendship and countless interesting talks with my animals. I know some people absolutely do not believe it can be done, or wouldn't want to do it. You may believe what you want, but after talking to Final Praise, I was hooked forever. Mary said animals talk in pictures. They don't hear the words, but rather the thoughts that go with them. I think that's why when you want to take your dog to the vet or groomer or give him a bath, you can't find him. Or, when you want to do something fun, your dog appears by your side without calling him. And perhaps that is why animal shelter pets are so grateful when they are adopted. These animals know more than what we might think.

I told her I was having problems with a foal. She asked me his name and what he looked like. I was a little disappointed. I'd expected she'd tell me something spectacular to impress me, but I gave her the information and she connected with him. She said he was confused, that he couldn't for the life of him figure out what in the world we were trying to do to him.

I thought we had been pretty clear on that point. A pull on the rope means go forward, and if someone pushes your rear that should make it even clearer. Stop when you hit the end of the rope–what more did he want? Mary explained it to him by showing him with her mind how a horse leads forward and stops, concentrating on the pressure on the top of his head when the rope tightened meaning he was to go forward. He said he under-stood, and I was excited to try it the next day. Mary said he was a nice colt, had a good mind and really wanted to cooperate if he could just figure out what the dickens we wanted.

The next day, Michal and I got out the equipment and went in the horse stall with some skepticism to get started on our mission. When we put the halter on his head, he stood still and didn't toss it at all. Michal attached the lead rope, and I led the mare out of the stall with Final following on his rope. He simply walked down the barn aisle to the arena–no stopping, pulling or running off. I was amazed. It was to be the first of many, many calls to Mary Long.

The colt was still a baby and had lots of learning to do, but now I had his mind and most things went along easier. I discovered that just talking to my animals through a communicator and telling them what I wanted them to do, didn't work any better than talking to a young child. Sometimes they would do it, sometimes not; sometimes they just forgot. Still it was a great addition to my training and a wonderful new way to enjoy my animals.

Now that my animals talked to me, I had a different perspective. They were thinking, feeling beings that could be upset, disappointed, sad, and probably all other emotions people exhibit. I felt that if I couldn't get the feel for a situation, I would talk to the animal through Mary and find out what was going on from his viewpoint. Sometimes it worked out beauti-fully; other times were failures, but I wouldn't stop trying to communicate with my animals. It was empowering.

Final Praise went on to become my best show weanling. He was unde-feated in four states with the exception of one second place. In the autumn of his first year, he started stumbling a little. At first I thought it was noth-ing alarming, but it continued and eventually affected his whole body. Vets were consulted; no one had a definitive diagnosis, although one thought it was Equine Protozoal Myelitis or EPM, a neurological disease spread by a protozoa in opossum feces and ingested by the horse in his food. We treated him with the prescribed anti-Protozoal medication, but it didn't work. I was heartbroken. Watching him struggle to get up in his stall was hard. Weeks later he couldn't get up unless someone pulled a lead rope attached to his halter to help him. I kept hoping that one of the suggested treatments would start to work, but time passed without results.

The fortunate thing was little Praise didn't show any sign of pain. He just couldn't move correctly. The only time he left his stall was to be turned loose in the inside arena where he could walk or try to run as he pleased and be as safe as possible. One evening he started to run in his usual shambling, staggery gait and fell in a heap on the ground. My heart was in my mouth as I ran to him. He lay still, barely breathing. He seemed to be unconscious. I sadly called the vet to come and euthanize him. Perhaps he had had some kind of seizure, but regardless, I knew my special little colt was leaving me.

Little Praise never regained consciousness before the vet arrived nearly an hour later. I sat by his side petting and talking to him with tears flowing down my cheeks. It doesn't matter how many animals you love and lose; it never gets any easier to say the final "Good-by."

Of all the colts I have ever had, he was the one I wanted to keep as a young stallion. He had it all—beauty, ability, a kind disposition, and wonderful bloodlines—and he was gone. I remembered that when my childhood horse, Smokey, was put down due to old age, my Mom who had what we might call second sight had seen Smokey's spirit leave his body. I was sure that I could feel Final Praise's spirit on the farm for a few days, running and playing like he couldn't when he was in his physical body, and then he was gone—both in spirit and body.

I know in my heart, soul and mind that there is Heaven for animals. Several good books are written on that subject. One of the early animal communicators, Beatrice Lydecker, wrote a book in 1979: *Stories the Animals Tell Me*. She relates the passing of her old Pomeranian, Blacky. "I felt Blacky relax in my arms, and as I stood there with tears streaming down my cheeks, I saw something so phenomenal I will remember it always. There, above the table, was the image of my Princess Royal, whom Blacky had helped raise and who had been his friend and companion for two years of his life. She was standing there waiting for him to join her. As he did, his body became whole and strong once more. He shook himself as he did after a bath, only this time he wasn't shaking water from his small frame. As he moved, his old body dropped from him in pieces, and he emerged as the beautiful, young, full-coated animal I had taken to live with me fourteen years earlier.

"It was like watching a butterfly emerge from a cocoon. When he stopped shaking himself, he began to dance around Princess Royal as he had used to, and she in turn nuzzled him affectionately. She wanted him to come with her and kept urging him to move. He stood looking at me for a moment, waiting to be released spiritually. Somehow I managed to say, I love you, Blacky. Go with Princess, now and have a good time. I'll see you later. As he said goodbye to me, I felt his extreme pleasure at being free. Then the image faded." Bea tells us animals do not fear death; it is their owners who have the problem of allowing their special friends to leave.

Another book I greatly enjoyed was *Will I See Fido in Heaven?* by Mary Buddemeyer-Porter. She shares Biblical scriptures to express this belief and has written several other books on the subject.

There is an ongoing debate among animal lovers, trainers, scientists and others who work with animals about attributing human feelings to them. It has a word: anthropomorphism. In sharing my experiences of communication with my animals, I am not advising treating your horse or other animal as you would a person. They are still an animal. They must behave themselves as such and be trained in kind and thoughtful ways. However, I believe that on another level of consciousness, they have feelings, thoughts and desires as we humans do. Getting in touch with this side of an animal adds new dimensions to our enjoyment, insights and ability to "train" them. But beware—if you talk to your horse or other animal friend yourself or through an animal communicator, you will never look at them the same way again!

CHAPTER TWENTY-EIGHT

The Writing on the Wall

By 1996, we weren't really on the fast track, but I was more than satisfied. Some of Hallelujah's babies were doing well in the show ring—proving that Hallelujah wasn't a fluke, and that he had something worthy to contribute to the gene pool. What type of mare he was mated with made a difference. Just as I had suspected, the looser-moving mares produced better show colts. Not that a colt necessarily had to be a show horse to be good; many of the colts were trail horses with nice gaits and sweet dispositions. That was important too, but because some were good show horses, it proved that his offspring would do the correct walking gait. We continued our winning ways in our five-state show area and decided to go to the 1996 International.

These judges weren't known to be as appreciative of non-sored horses as the ones in '93 and '95, but we thought we'd give it a go. We got two second placings and one of them was in our very own Amateur Owned and Trained class, which was a very big disappointment. His gait wasn't getting any worse— the sored horses were being placed above him. Hallelujah performed his usual beautiful canter and we won the Plantation Canter class, probably because the sored pleasure horses had a hard time cantering. Because their front feet hurt when one landed on the ground, the reaction was to quickly snatch it back up. This worked for gaiting, but sometimes made a shambles of cantering. We didn't bother staying for any Championship classes, as I could foresee how that would probably end. It wasn't fun being beaten by horses trained by dubious means. Best come home, save our money and avoid more frustration.

The following year, 1997, we bred more mares and got eleven in foal. We had a good show year at our local shows and I rebred Black Cashmier. She had foaled the year before and produced a stud colt who was some sort of genetic throwback. He was solid black, pretty, and had really small, beautiful ears. When I first saw him and his gorgeous ears I was thrilled with his beauty. As time went on, I became less so. Cashmier had big floppy ears, so did Final Praise—a trait that often indicates a quiet horse. Hallelujah's were ordinary, pretty ears and I wondered at the time where this new little black colt got those exceptionally refined ears.

Odyssey was a nasty colt. I had wanted to keep him as a stallion, but at two years of age after he reared in his stall and clipped my eighty-four-year-old stall cleaner's scalp, I gelded him. He never turned out to be anything great. He was lazy and had a bad attitude; it was obvious he didn't even try. I tried talking to him via Mary, the animal communicator, and he indicated he really didn't care what I wanted.

That year, we tried the International again. I was even more concerned with the judge's roster this time, and rightfully so as it turned out. After starting out with an eighth place in the first class, things didn't get much better. Hallelujah got another eighth in the next class and I was pretty discouraged. Our Amateur Owned and Trained classes were yet to come and I hoped for better. Sadly for us, a new horse had entered our usual group of exhibitors.

A woman with a big, black mare who heretofore had not shown at the International entered our class. She showed at the Celebration and always did very well. She stabled her horse at a sore big lick training barn during the show. She was an amateur, but as far as I was concerned, knew the tricks of the trade. She got the blue, another horse got second, and Hallelujah and I ended up with third place. The same thing happened in the other Amateur Owned and Trained class, and again we packed up and went home, even more disgruntled than ever before. In '94, when we had our other bad year, it was because Hallelujah was lame. There was no real reason this time. It wasn't the horse's fault, but was an indication of things to come.

I wasn't being a bad sport about losing. I knew Hallelujah was not the best plantation show horse in the country. If I was beaten by a sound-trained competitor, it would be unfortunate for my ambitions, but I wouldn't complain. Having others cheat, break the law and put a suffering horse in the ring was another matter. It took the fun and enjoyment out of the whole venture.

CHAPTER TWENTY-NINE

Nugget

Lady Called Coin, or Nugget as we called the regal mare, was truly a magnificent animal. The first time I saw her was at a horse show. I just stood and stared, then went over to touch her. I was drooling, I am sure. She was elegant—a glossy, dark-chocolate brown with long legs, a trait I loved in horses, and she had the softest brown eyes. You could tell she had a great disposition and was willing to please. I had a lot of great horses myself, so I wasn't just a novice horse fan falling in love with a pretty horse.

Eventually I talked to Connie, the owner, telling her if she ever wanted to sell her mare, to *please* let me know first. She said it was very unlikely she would sell. Connie loved her horses and was a very responsible horse owner. If something happened to them and they couldn't show, or they just got old, she kept them anyway. Since she didn't have a farm, all her horses were boarded or with trainers, and this could get expensive.

Nugget was around four years old when I first saw her. Shortly after that she began having some knee problems and the trainer and Connie thought it might be a good thing to retire her before more damage occurred. She was very young to be having this difficulty, but Connie was a good owner, and she didn't want to injure her further. I bought her as a brood mare—a horse to mate with Praise Hallelujah. Part of the deal was Connie would get the first baby, and I would get the others. She also wrote a purchase contract stating that if I ever wanted to sell her, I must give her right of first refusal. All horses should be that lucky.

Nugget had her first baby, a filly named Gifted. She was choice! When she was weaned, Connie moved her from our farm to a trainer who showed her successfully. During her yearling year she developed a bone disorder causing her ankles to swell and eventually she couldn't walk well on them. This was extremely disappointing because Gifted had been a fantastic weanling and yearling show filly. Connie moved her to another farm and had various veterinarians work with her. The treatments eventually got her sound enough to be a pasture horse, but she could never be ridden.

I rebred Nugget back to Praise Hallelujah, and another filly was born about a year later. This filly also developed the same bone problem. I rebred Nugget a third time to Praise Hallelujah. There was no problem with the birth, but the little colt had a great deal of trouble breathing. He was gasping big gulps of air like a drowning person. I was devastated. Now what was the problem? I cleared his lungs as best I could by wiping his nose, opened his mouth and clearing out the mucus, but no change.

I called the vet.

Night-time foaling meant I would get an "on call" vet, whose turn it was to take the night hours, and he could be anywhere in the county. Fortunately, he was at home and came quickly, but it still seemed to take forever as I sat stroking the distressed foal and listened to his wheezing. The vet tried to clear his airway more but nothing helped. He listened with his stethoscope and found a very serious heart murmur. The blood was gurgling back and forth, not being pumped through. His problem was not his lungs but his poor little heart.

There really was no hope for the baby, and he was euthanized rather than allowing him to struggle for air until his oxygen-deprived system gave out, or trying heroic measures that likely would fail. All this time, Nugget was worried, but being the lady she was, didn't get in the way. She trusted we would save her foal. I decided I should leave the foal in Nugget's stall so she would realize it was dead, rather than taking it out right away, and the vet agreed. It was winter and cold enough that the foal wouldn't decompose quickly.

It seemed to take three days of separation at weaning time to convince my mares and foals they could live without each other, so I had it in my mind to leave her baby that long if I had to, but I was hoping one day would suffice. She stood over the foal all night, eating her hay and some grain which I placed beside the baby. Morning chore time came, and I checked on her. She was still standing there. She had eaten and drunk but was staying at her post. Okay, day two went by and she still devotedly stayed with her baby. Day three, she was still there and she had started to paw at it to make it get up, pushing it out into the center of her large foaling stall.

Obviously, leaving the foal with her any longer was not going to help the mare, and I had Bob take it out. Nugget grieved, looked for her baby and called to it just like at weaning time. Eventually she settled in with her usual routine. I promised myself I would *never* breed her again. I called Mary, the animal communicator, and we talked to Nugget. She mourned her baby and wanted him to have a name. She didn't want him to be forgotten. I named him Nugget's Prince of Praise, and she was content. No one could definitely tell me why Nugget had such bad luck with her babies. There were several theories, one being that she and Praise Hallelujah genetically did not cross, but it didn't matter to me. I was through breeding her.

During these years something very exciting had happened to Nugget. Through supplements made especially for joints, joint injections of special ingredients to help her joints recover, and veterinarian chiropractic treatments, she was able to become a show horse once again. She showed in-between her pregnancies and sometimes during the early part of them and did very well for herself, getting many blue ribbons and awards.

After the trauma for us all with Nugget's Prince of Praise, I concluded we would simply show; no need for more babies. The decision felt right to me. However, one day when I was talking to Nugget through Mary Long, the mare told me she really wanted to have another baby. Horrors! How could I explain that *that* was not going to happen? This is what I mean about seeing your animals differently once you talk to them. I was the owner, the boss. *I* decided when and who would have foals, right?

All horses have their own personalities: some bold and bossy, others quiet and unassuming like Nugget. Surely her lady-like personality would understand and comply with my wishes. I explained why she shouldn't have a foal, but she wanted to try again anyway. I thought it would be absolutely too hard on both of us if she lost another, but she didn't care. I guess in her own way, when something was important, she could be stubborn, too.

One year later, after feeling guilty now and then about not letting her have another chance at motherhood, I bred her to My Vision, a pretty, black stallion I'd recently purchased. I was hoping, betting, and praying that a different stallion would make a difference in the outcome. She conceived right away; I'm sure she wanted to get pregnant before I had a change of heart.

About ten months later I began checking Nugget's udder and teats. Usually before a mare foals, her milk comes in and makes the udder large and sometimes milk leaks out. I had been checking her for the signs and there were none. I wasn't worried though, she would have her baby when she was ready. She was in the big foaling stall at night, and I had removed her from the pasture with the other horses during the day so whenever she delivered the baby it would be safe. She was two weeks away according to my records.

One night as I made my usual before-bed check, I noticed her udder was larger, I could get some milk out, and she seemed a little sweaty. But since delivery was two weeks away, I decided she was slowly getting into form. However to be cautious, I positioned the birth alarm around her girth area and went to bed, only to be awakened in half an hour by the alarm. (By now I had gotten a foaling monitor which beeped a raucous noise in my bedroom when the mare gave signs of foaling. These monitors are a much better system than going out to the barn every two hours and hoping you hit the proper timing.)

I was in attendance at the birth again; everything went normally and Nugget presented us with a beautiful, black filly. The large filly had very long elegant legs like her daddy and mother, and she was unusually awkward in getting them under control to stand.

After Nugget had the baby, I called Bob awakening him from deep sleep to come help her stand up. She was too heavy for me. I always hated to watch the babies' first few hours after birth. They struggle to stand, fall over, get up, and fall again. If I think all is well, I leave and let them sort it out, but this filly's legs were so long I worried. After a safe birth, I positively didn't want anything to happen to her now. I was exhausted, even more so than Nugget who was so proud and pleased! You could almost see her smile. I talked Bob into staying with her for an hour until she got her land legs, and went to bed quickly falling into a deep, dreamless sleep.

Vision of Sugar Plums was an adorable filly. By the following morning she was strong and active. She found momma's dinner pail and all seemed to be going well. Sugar Plum was healthy, but she was always nursing, butting Nugget's udder more often than was usual for a foal. After a day of this behavior, I checked the udder—which didn't seem as full to me as it should have been. The filly was nursing often and pushing her head into the udder because Nugget wasn't making enough milk. Sugar Plum was hungry and irritated!

Sometimes, as my mother used to say, "God moves in mysterious ways." One of the possible reasons for all of Nugget's babies' problems was her milk didn't have the proper minerals for a fast-growing foal. This wouldn't have explained the heart murmur, but the explanation fit for Nugget's other two fillies and their bone problems. One of my horse friends told me she'd had the same bone problem with one of her mare's foals. They all had to have surgery, but fortunately for her, all turned out to be rideable. The only one that didn't have a problem had nursed not only from her own mother, but also from another unusually generous nursing mare. She was the first to tell me Nugget's milk could be to blame.

Now, here was Sugar Plum, not getting *any* milk to speak of. We'd have to supplement feed her. Bob nailed some boards across a corner of the stall, just high enough to let Sugar Plum under and keep the mare out. Because the foal was hungry, it wasn't long before she was finding and eating the special milk replacer pellets for orphan foals. Since she couldn't fill her tummy with mom's milk, she'd have to eat the properly-designed foal feed. If she'd had plenty of mother's milk, she wouldn't have wanted the pellets, and we never would have found out for sure the problem was in fact Nugget's milk. Sugar Plum enjoyed nursing from Nugget until she was weaned but never got much milk, just mother's love.

Sugar Plum grew normally, having only a slight difficulty when she was a year old, but a feed change fixed the problem. She had her sire and mom's long legs and great temperament. She and Nugget lived happily together in the pasture along with the other horses; in fact, a little too happily. It was as though they were never completely weaned from each other. When I took Nugget out for a trail ride, she behaved in her usual lady-like manner, but it was apparent her mind was elsewhere. She had a grown child back at the barn who needed mothering. She guarded and protected Sugar from other horses even when it wasn't necessary. Eventually I sold Sugar to one of my boarders, and she moved to the other side of the barn, another pasture, and finally, after three years, weaning was accomplished.

Every now and then I think I hear Nugget whisper in my mind, "What do you think about having another baby?" but I tell her we both are retired from raising baby horses. We will leave well enough alone.

CHAPTER THIRTY

Cookie's Story

Life was good. My stallion was working, showing and breeding well, and several of my other horses were also doing great in competition. The boarding business was booming. We actually were making money with the farm for a change. I was extremely busy with the training and breeding end of things and wouldn't have minded if life quieted down somewhat; but a coming event was about to add more, not less, drama to my life.

One spring morning in 1997, I answered the phone. It was Ralph, Hallelujah's former trainer. "Rose," he said without the usual chit chat, "there's one of Hallelujah's fillies that I want to tell you about."

My first thought was, "Don't tell me she is for sale. I don't need any more horses!"

He went on to say that another trainer that he knew quite well had a filly by Praise Hallelujah he wanted to sell as he was having a problem getting her to gait; all she wanted to do was pace. He asked Ralph to come look at her. When Ralph arrived, the trainer literally dragged the young horse out of the stall. She was a small two-year-old chestnut filly, under 15 hands high. To cure a pacy horse, or "fix" one to walk, unscrupulous trainers use more soring and heavier chains on the front feet. This trainer was known to me as one who used plenty of chemicals. The back of her front ankles were raw; but nonetheless, chains were placed around her pasterns. She needed ample encouragement to even move under saddle. The trainer didn't sic the dogs on her, but Ralph had seen him use that method of getting his sore horses to move forward. He told the trainer he didn't think she was pacy; his training was all wrong for the filly. Ralph came home and immediately called me.

Ralph knew Hallelujah and some of his offspring and guessed the filly was too natural to respond to soring. If one doctors a natural moving horse, all one does is ruin it; you can't "make" it better. That is why the breeders of the new type Walking Horses were tending towards more pacing blood in the pedigrees.

When Ralph told me about the mare, I thought I could ignore her plight. I didn't want any more horses, especially one that wasn't gaiting correctly, and I thought her price was high. Nonetheless, I called the trainer the next day and tried to get him to come down on the cost. He held firm, and I let another couple days go by. It was getting harder and harder to forget about the little mare's plight. The next day I called Ralph and told him I was going to make a decision that was not based on good business sense but rather on my heart. I was going to buy her. I couldn't have one of Hallelujah's babies in such a place or condition. I called the trainer and said I would purchase her for his price. Then I heard more bad news.

"We took her hind shoes off and rode her on the gravel road trying to get her to gait, and now she is lame. Do you still want her?" he asked. Riding a barefoot Walking Horse on gravel is another ploy to make a pacy horse square up. If they are sore on the rear feet they can't swing them forward and put as much weight on them as normal so it shortens the pace stride. A horse's hoof is like a fingernail. The part of the nail that we cut off is like the part of the hoof that gets the nails in to hold on a shoe. It doesn't hurt. Like our fingernail, the hoof has a sensitive part called the quick. If we cut our fingernails too close, it hurts. Can you imagine walking on something that hurts like that? At this point I hardly could choke back tears and felt sick to my stomach. I said, "Yes, I still want her." and left it up to Ralph to work out getting the little mare to his barn.

The trainer delivered her that same night. He handed her rope to Ralph and looking somewhat embarrassed, climbed back in his truck and left. The mare hobbled three-legged into the barn. As soon as she was in the stall, she lay down. Ralph is a rather tough customer. He likes, maybe even loves his horses, but he isn't very demonstrative. They work, get fed and cared for, maybe even receive a pat on the neck, but there are no apples, treats, hugs or mushy words; however, this young horse's plight even got to Ralph. When he called to relate the event of her coming to his barn, I swear I heard a catch in his voice. He was mad, too; angry that such a thing would be done to any horse, let alone one of Hallelujah's. Ralph had a big soft spot in his heart for Hallelujah; they had been a great team, if even just for a short while.

I don't remember what the mare's given name was, but it didn't have "Praise" in it. A very large percentage of his offspring either had Praise in their names or had a Biblical name. Of course, she had to have one too. I renamed her Cash in on Praise after both her mother and her sire. We needed a barn name for her, and one soon became evident as she showed a fondness for the cookies Betsy, Ralph's wife, shared with her.

The vet suspected an abscess in Cookie's hind foot, caused by a piece of gravel from the road being driven into it. After much foot soaking and pain medication, a piece of gravel worked its way up to the coronary band of her foot and oozed its way out. Soon the plucky little mare was getting frisky in her stall and became impatient for her food. Her bright eyes sparkled when someone walked by. Cookie was resurrected. Now she was ready for training again and by June she was all set for her first horse show. Cookie was a picture; she was groomed to within an inch of her life and her natural ability came to the fore as she won her first blue ribbon in the 2-Year-Old Class. We had quite a celebration.

Ralph and Cookie did very well that summer, and when fall rolled around bringing with it the International Horse Show in Tennessee, I wanted to go. Ralph didn't participate in that show because he always went to the big Celebration which was just a few weeks later, and he didn't care to make the long trip more than once. However, the Celebration held more prestige and he had gone to it for years. But he agreed to go to the International this year with Cookie, and we made our plans. He'd drive his truck, taking no horses, and we would take our truck and trailer, stop by his place, pick up Cookie to join Hallelujah and go on to Tennessee. Everything proceeded as planned except for one problem—Cookie was a trailer kicker.

As we drove down the highway, we heard loud bangs and the normally steady gooseneck trailer would jolt a little. It was especially bad whenever we had to stop. We came to a standstill several times to check on her and be sure she hadn't gotten a hind foot stuck over or in something. We were unquestionably happy to pull onto the showgrounds.

It was 1998, and as the years had passed, more and more sored pleasure horses were being exhibited, especially at the big shows, and the International was no exception. The show was divided in two parts—the first days were for the pleasure horses, and later the big lick Walkers would arrive and show. Because of this division, our stabling area which was the same ever since our second International, didn't house sored horses so far as we knew. There were no draped stalls or private grooming areas where the sored horses were doctored. If a person sored his horses, he tried to do it in secret, even though everyone around knew what was going on behind those curtained areas. We knew a lot of the folks, many from different areas of the country as well as Tennessee. Over time they had become once-a-year friends. This year something was going to be different.

One of the padded big lick horse trainers also trained pleasure horses, and he was from our Indiana area. I actually liked him as a person, and his wife was gracious and enjoyable company. He was also a judge and for some strange reason, he awarded good placings to a lot of natural, sound-moving pleasure horses in the ring. A sored-*looking* pleasure horse with vastly exaggerated front and rear movement, or one that was most lame, didn't get his nod. He'd been one of the judges at the Celebration when I showed Hallelujah. He hadn't seen us make our canter screw up and had tied us third, a great placing in that class with many sored pleasure horses. Unfortunately, he had the reputation of putting quite sore pleasure horses *in* the ring. This year he shared our stall area and was in our aisle. To walk to the arena area to watch, get concessions or visit the restrooms, the easiest route took us by his stalls.

Cookie wasn't in her best form; I think the 7-hour trip was stressful on her, especially with her frequent kicking of the rear of the trailer. She was stiff moving and if I looked closely, seemed a little off in her rear stride. My good friend Carolyn was a horse muscle therapist and she always did wonders with Hallelujah by muscle stretching, massage and spinal manipulations. I was disappointed Ralph didn't want her to work on Cookie but he was the trainer so Cookie had to limber up the best she could by her workouts. One of the bad things about our stall area was that the horses stood on concrete. This in itself always made the horses stiff, and the sawdust bedding wasn't enough of a cushion to alleviate the problem.

Ralph showed her in the first class getting a third-place ribbon. It wasn't their best showing. My daughter Chessa showed her in the larger Lady's Amateur class also getting a third place. She looked a little better in that class, and Chessa was justifiably delighted. Hallelujah did his best, getting two second placings and one third. Considering the sored competition, it was good enough. The biggest trouble was caused by the trainer who shared our aisle.

Cookie and Chessa
Photo by Jack Green

In the 1980s, my early years of showing my mare Angel, Xanadu and the horses of that era, I saw sored big lick Walking Horses competing at our shows, but we had little in common with them, their trainers or owners. We didn't fraternize. We watched them compete in relative acceptance of their way of going and even their training/soring methods because it was just the way it was. I didn't know how it was done, just that the padded show horses were different with their stacks, chains and tail sets which propped their tails up. They were unnatural, weird, and we didn't really pay attention.

When Hallelujah entered my life, I saw soring up close. I learned how it was done. I watched the DQP inspections of competing pleasure horses I knew were sored and hoped they would get caught—but usually they didn't. Different inspection methods were introduced by the USDA such as thermography which detected heat caused by the soring chemicals. The trainers devised other methods such as pressure shoeing—putting objects under the shoes to cause pain when the horse set his foot down. Sometimes right before a show, the horses had their feet trimmed to the blood before the shoes were nailed onto their hooves. These tactics couldn't always be detected and were much more painful for the horse as there was never any relief. Some Walking Horses got colic, a severe and painful abdominal illness, and died. Owners and trainers would swear soring or causing pain to the horse didn't cause colic, but many others didn't agree, including the horse insurance companies, many of which wouldn't insure a Walking Horse especially if it was a show animal.

Our classes at the International would take three days and on the second day we observed, up close and personal, the effect of soring upon one of God's creatures. The mare was tied in the aisle by two ropes, one on each side of the aisle. Her head, instead of being tied up, was being *held* up because she was leaning into the ties. She placed her front feet back toward her middle to alleviate some of the pain, and she shoved her rear feet toward the front—the typical foot in a bucket stance of the sored horse. Her belly muscles were tight and drawn up. She looked totally miserable. If we were to walk in that direction, we had to pass by her. My comment to Michal and to anyone who would listen was, "If I had a horse that looked like that, I would be calling a veterinarian; I certainly would not be *causing* it to feel like that!"

I was furious, sick at heart—and sick to my stomach. This just wasn't right. Of course it hadn't been right for about 40 years, but it had finally gotten to my soul. It was my time to grieve. The plight of that poor mare and many like her was the reason for all the curtained off stall areas at the shows. Most trainers didn't want the public to witness this atrocity, but here was this pathetic animal in view for all to see. Somehow this blatant disrespect made the whole situation worse. Was this now such an accepted practice that trainers didn't even try to hide it?

I observed the mare during the morning before the afternoon and evening classes began. The question was—what to do about it? The show DQPs were not visible; the government inspectors weren't there as yet; and we didn't see the trainer either, but talking to him wouldn't do any good anyway. I decided to go to show management and register a complaint. I was afraid nothing much would come of it, but it was the best I could think of to do. A little later the mare was put back into her stall at the bequest of management. Of course it was much too little for either the large problem of soring or for that horse. This affair put a pall on the rest of the show for all of us and burst our bubble of enjoyment.

A horse trainer I knew, who wished to remain unidentified and I shall call Henry, related a similar but even worse incident that had occurred to him. One year at a big southern show, Henry was asked by another trainer to take his horse out of the stall a couple times a day, lead him around to limber him up, and put some salve on his front feet, as he had to leave for part of the day. Henry agreed, but doing the favor was actually downright disagreeable. He had to drag the horse out of the stall and then couldn't get him to move. Forget about limbering him up; the horse wouldn't walk. As he was trying to pull the horse along, another trainer walked by and remarked, "Got him in a bind, huh?" Henry hastened to tell him the horse wasn't his, but the other trainer just grinned. What was the big deal anyway? There were dozens just like that horse on the show grounds. Henry said he was mightily embarrassed and quickly put the horse back in his stall.

When the horse's trainer returned, Henry told him that the horse couldn't walk and when he touched his front feet to put salve on them, he reared up on his hind ones. The trainer assured Henry that *he* would get the horse to walk. Later Henry saw the horse being whipped with a long black snake whip; sure enough, the trainer had gotten his horse to move. The horse showed later that night. How in the world did that horse get through inspection and into the show ring?

We stayed the third day so Ralph could show Cookie in the Two-Year-Old Championship class. I'd already decided I wouldn't show Hallelujah any more at that show. I really just wanted to go home. My nerves were a wreck, and I had started crying at any time and any place. I know people wondered what in the world was wrong with Rose Miller. Cookie put in a really rotten performance that night. She was noticeably stiff and sore looking. Standing on the concrete was really getting to her. She truly needed a spa and a good chiropractor.

She received next to last place and it was a fitting end to an awful experience. We packed up and headed for home with my tears still flowing. We never went back to the International or the Celebration where many sored pleasure as well as big lick horses were so prevalent.

Ralph had Cookie for another month and showed her at a big show in Ohio where she excelled and received three blues from what I considered to be a sore-horse judge. We said our thanks to Ralph and headed for home with our little Cookie. Her days of professional training were finished. After the required waiting period was over, she'd join Hallelujah in the Amateur Owned and Trained division.

Cookie was very talented, and as Walking Horse people say, "She had a great back end." Her conformation allowed her to shove those hind feet underneath herself in fine fashion and she had good lift to her front feet. There was one fall show left in the season, and I planned to take her and compete without the aid of a trainer.

I had a month to accomplish my goal. The horse chiropractor was called; massage and liniment were the norm of the day. My farrier trimmed her front feet a little shorter so she could manage them better and we used a size smaller shoe. Sometimes bigger isn't better. I hoped it would work and that I wouldn't humiliate myself at our first show. I was using the dressage training methods I had been taught by Mr. Sherman, and she was learning to balance herself better. She would never be a big horse; in fact, she never quite reached 15 hands, but under saddle she looked powerful. I called her the "little horse with the big heart." The show was a success. Showing only in 2 two-year-old classes, she got a blue and a reserve (second place) ribbons. We returned home very pleased.

Her winter training went well; as a three-year-old, she got stronger and her gait was even better. I began teaching her to canter. She seemed to have inherited her sire's lovely slow cadenced canter, and it came easy for her. In April we went to a prestigious show in Ohio; the first of the season. Sored horses would be competing, but the judge was one known to me as a sound-horse judge. He awarded Cookie four blues—a first place for each class entered including a canter class, and she had been ridden by three different riders. She wasn't just talented; she was phenomenal!

The judge told me after the show that Cookie was the "best horse on the grounds." But for me, my family and my horses it was the calm before the storm.

CHAPTER THIRTY-ONE

Consequences

In the fall of 1998, when I returned home from the International Show with my heart, mind and soul in grief and turmoil over the plight of the Walking Horse, I knew I had to do something—but what? The problem was enormous and numerous outspoken people also incensed by the practice of soring, had been trying to change the system for years but to no avail. The problem had many facets, but the obvious soring and consequent suffering of horses was worse in some localities than others. If you stayed out of Tennessee and Kentucky and surrounding southern areas, soring wasn't as blatant hence people weren't as concerned.

The first decade (in the 80s) of my horse competitions with Xanadu and my other horses of that era, was in Michigan, Illinois, and Indiana where very few horses were sored. I was a young woman with a family starting a new venture with a totally different kind of horse and concerns enough of my own. Soring wasn't my issue. I wasn't uncaring. I was uneducated and busy.

The second decade of show-ring competitions showcased Praise Hallelujah and his offspring. At this time I was very aware of soring and its effects although I didn't do it and didn't allow my horse trainer to do it. Along with many of my fellow sound-horse competitors, I wanted to demonstrate to audiences and horse owners at the big prestigious shows that a well-bred, talented and humanely-trained horse could compete with the best of the sored ones and still win. Many times we did. That was my mission statement against soring.

After the 1998 International, things changed for me. I realized I wasn't making a statement anymore. The trainers and owners weren't impressed with my sound horse. Many thought I sored him anyway, albeit not very well. The soring of the pleasure horse had reached a new, higher level of acceptance and it was demoralizing.

What could I do, I wondered, that had not already been done? It wasn't as though the soring issue had been ignored by the sincere Tennessee Walking Horse loving populace. Several organizations had been formed such as Friends of the Sound Horse (FOSH) and the Sound Horse Organization, but it was like fighting a raging forest fire. These groups were vocal in their complaints and politically active, but the big Walking Horse industry had a lot of political clout and fought even the government (USDA) attempts to stop soring.

I had no fresh, ingenious plan, but I knew a Higher Power had to be asked for help. This was bigger than mere mortal beings. The next day I wrote a letter to many of my horse-show friends asking them to join me in thought at a certain time on a special day for heavenly help for our horses' plight. Many responded positively.

Months later I learned that just days after I wrote my letter— the end of August 1998, a group of sixteen people gathered by invitation only, for a secret meeting in Murfreesboro, Tennessee, during the Celebration to discuss the soring issue. Many had horses participating at that show and were concerned for the welfare of their animals if it became known they were meeting to discuss the wrong treatment of the Walking Horse.

In October of that same year, fifty people from different states including Pennsylvania, Maryland, Virginia, Ohio, Indiana, Kentucky, Tennessee, and California met at the Adams Mark Motel at the Indianapolis airport and organized the National Walking Horse Association (NWHA). I am a lifetime member. The NWHA goal: to license judges and DQPs in order to promote sound versus sored Tennessee Walking Horses in the show ring. To date, this organization has had a lot of clout by affiliating with many horse shows and receiving the monies that would otherwise go to supporting the large national organization that inherently supported soring.

I had retired from judging the Walking Horse's National Horse Show Commission (NHSC), or "Commission" shows in 1994. With the organization of NWHA, I was asked by Don Bell, the first Director of Operations, to judge for the new organization, and I accepted. Later I served on

NWHA's Judge's Committee and wrote articles on judging for the National News. It has been a fulfilling undertaking.

NWHA has a *zero* tolerance for soring, unlike the Operating Plans drawn up by the Walking Horse industry, whose goal was for the USDA to be as lenient as possible on trainers and owners. Government officials attending NWHA sponsored and inspected shows were heard to comment they enjoyed coming to NWHA shows. In fact the USDA inspectors seldom appeared at NWHA officiated events. They felt confident those horses were competently inspected. Only a tiny percentage of sored pleasure horses even tried to compete at NWHA sanctioned events.

The NWHA office moved to the Kentucky Horse Park in 2006. It is an organization whose time has come. Fighting the soring of our horses is a process, not an event. Finally after years of having no alternative for showing my horses, now I could go to NWHA affiliated competitions and so could hundreds of other horse owners. Over the seven-year span I continued to compete at these NWHA events, many of us were saddened by the continuing lack of progress in the inspection and judging of the many National Horse Show Commission affiliated shows. Part of the battle was won, but the war continued.

CHAPTER THIRTY-TWO

Sharon

"Hello, Mom." my oldest daughter's voice quavered. "It is breast cancer."

Time stood still.

I remember exactly where I was and what I was doing to this very day.

Sharon had been a most precocious child, driven to succeed in all she did. She was my first horse buddy. Maybe even the reason our family ended up on a horse farm. She was beautiful, smart and healthy. She was physically active, muscular and fit from competing in triathlons, 10K races and aerobic competitions. There was no breast cancer in our family; she did not smoke, drink or use birth control pills. Breast cancer surely wasn't possible. But it was.

Hal and I had much to be grateful for. We had four wonderful children who had never caused parental alarm; we had no financial worries, and we enjoyed our beautiful farm in the country with Dad, Mom and my sister's family living within feet of us. Because life was good and we trusted God that life would stay that way, when things went suddenly awry, it was doubly devastating. I hate to admit it, but it sorely tried my faith.

My mother, 87 years old, was in failing health. But this news from Sharon–my mind, numbed and unprepared, couldn't fathom it as truth. Surely she'd beat it, surely. My next thought was that without a doubt further diagnosis would prove *her* case could be easily treated. Sharon was so healthy and vital. She would be one of the survivors of this deadly disease.

As a family, we discussed telling my mother the news and decided to postpone it. She still lived in her own home with Dad which was next door to both my sister and me. A few weeks after Sharon's diagnosis, Mom who had been a very big part of all her grandchildren's lives, passed away quietly one night without being told of her oldest granddaughter's illness.

Mom and Dad

Sharon's cancer turned out to be inflammatory breast disease, one of the most deadly cancers. She had the usual treatment of surgery and chemo and came to the farm when she was strong enough to see the horses she and I loved. Her marriage and work had taken her to the west side of Chicago so we hadn't seen as much of each other in later years as we would have liked. Sharon hadn't been able to be involved with the horses after her marriage, but she still loved them.

I remember the first day Sharon came home to ride. Her hair was chemo short and at times stuck straight up like a punk rock star's, but her smile shone through and her eyes sparkled. Sharon rode Praise Hallelujah in the outside arena, cantering him around and around and around with that same look of pure joy I had seen on her face as a young girl riding Sir and later, Delight. I was glad for those brief times when I could still bestow happiness upon her with a horse.

Next to my trust in God and the love Hal and I shared, I had my horses. They were a great comfort. They occupied my hands, feet and mind during this trying time. When I was a young girl living on our Pennsylvania farm, I often discussed life with my pet Jersey cow Buttercup. She was the one who heard about any unhappiness, real or imagined.

Now I cried in my horses' presence about loss and feared loss, or I saddled one of my favorites and galloped down the trail with the wind in my face, or I let a fast running walk take my mind to happier places and times. Just brushing one of the horses was relaxing. My mind went into standby mode. My horses were a constant—they were always there for me. The barn was a peaceful place. It smelled of hay, grain, and fresh-cut apples—even the smell of fresh horse manure had its own comforting pungent odor.

The barn was also the place I worked. Feeding and caring for twenty-five or more horses each day wasn't optional. After being awakened from a sound sleep in the wee small hours of the morning by my daughter sobbing in pain at the other end of the telephone, my sleep was over, as was my peace of mind. But I had to pull myself together and care for the animals who counted on me.

By nature, I am a "fixer." I had a lot of education in the health field, using alternative treatments such as herbs and vitamins, and I went to work reading everything I could find about building the immune system of a cancer patient. When Sharon called with various symptoms, many times I suggested something to help. But it was frustrating to both of us. Her cancer thwarted all our efforts.

Finally one day she said a little sharply, "Mom, I don't want you to try and fix me. I just want you to listen and sympathize. Just tell me you are sorry and cry with me."

That sounded easy, but in reality it was very hard. Part of the way I coped with the very probable death of my daughter was to search for help. Although I never quit looking and searching, I needed to learn a mom lesson. Sometimes just being there and shedding tears along with her was enough.

CHAPTER THIRTY-THREE

Devastation

After Sharon was diagnosed with breast cancer, Michal, who had been my show and riding buddy for twenty years, lost interest in the horses. That perhaps occurred because most of her emotional energy was spent making trips to Chicago to spend time with Sharon. It was understandable but another loss for me. We had been a fixture on the show scene. The 1998 International with Cookie was our last show together as a family. One morning the following spring after I had finished feeding the horses, the barn phone rang.

"Hi, Rose. You don't know me, but I have a fifteen-year-old daughter, Erica, who loves horses. Do you need anyone to help you? You wouldn't need to pay her. If she could just spend time in the barn, it would be wonderful."

I lost count of the many calls like this one I received over the years. People saw a farm and horses and they had a child–usually a girl–and hoped I would like free help. I always said "No," thinking it would be more trouble than it was worth, and I had family involved anyway. This time it was like an answer to a prayer. I was excited at the prospect of having another young person to share my love of horses. The next day Erica arrived at the barn and over time carved a place in my heart. She was a good student and I taught her as I had my children. Soon she was indispensable.

The fun and excitement of owning and showing Cookie, our fabulous little mare, continued into the summer months. Cookie was all the more precious to me because she had entered my life a few months before Sharon's breast cancer diagnosis. The mare provided distraction as well as pleasure. In July, Erica and I went to a small local show; we showed Cookie the first day with good results. The second day was hotter, nearly 90 degrees, there was very little breeze and the stalls weren't furnished with electrical outlets to allow for fans. Erica was riding the little mare in a juvenile class for young people under 17. Cookie started out reasonably well but after turning around to go the second direction of the ring, she seemed to run out of steam and went slower and slower. Finally she just stopped and stood still on the track. Erica looked at me. I called over and told her to ask to be excused.

My first thoughts were that it was a hot day, her stall was hot, and she just had gotten overheated in the show ring, but I certainly wondered. I had seen big lick horses just stop in the ring, but they had reason to. Many of them seemed to really struggle to make it around with their big shoes, chains and sore feet. We hosed her off to cool her down and used a long extension cord to hook up a fan to cool her off more. We went home soon after, but that episode definitely spoiled a nice show. The rest of the show season which ended in October, continued without a hitch. Cookie ended her year by competing at five shows and winning 14 blue ribbons.

Cookie and Erica

Winter came and one morning in January when I went to the barn to feed, I could see Cookie was ill. She wouldn't eat, not even apples, her favorite treat. She stood with her head down and looked miserable. I called our usual farm veterinarian. He looked at her and concluded that she didn't have colic, but something was very wrong and I should consider taking her somewhere quickly. Dr. Brandt's clinic in Niles, Michigan, was my animal hospital. I preferred him over either the Purdue or Michigan State animal hospitals, plus he was only an hour away and the others were three. We loaded her into the trailer; she was a little unsteady and seemed to be failing right before my eyes.

Dr. Brandt looked grave as he gave her a preliminary examination, taking blood for tests and listening to her vital signs. We left her there hooked up to several bags of intravenous fluids, her head hanging and barely standing up. Dr. Brandt said it didn't look good, but he would do what he could and would contact me as soon as he knew anything. We drove home in silence. What on earth could have happened to that wonderful little mare—and so quickly, too? I'd never had a horse ailment that affected the animal this fast or so completely.

Several hours later the vet called to give me the disastrous news. Cookie was in complete liver failure, and there was no hope she could recover. She was euthanized to end her misery. My little Cookie, was just several months over four years old, and she was gone; a promising show career ended and one of the great horse loves of my life snuffed out. Why?

The next day, when I felt I could talk about Cookie with Dr. Brandt, he told me a creature can live without a lot of their liver—it can be damaged by one means or another—but when the critical point is reached, life cannot be sustained. Apparently Cookie's liver had been in trouble for some time. There are no defining signs, but being cranky and out of sorts—just not feeling up to par—is one. That had to be the reason for the inside and the outside of my barn being marked up with scores of Cookie's hind hoof prints, and why she continuously kicked the trailer.

There were no earlier symptoms for which to consult a vet. It was natural for me to second guess my care. I should have had blood work done when she didn't seem quite right, or after her quitting in the show ring, I should have called the vet. She never seemed actually sick, and if an owner called the veterinarian for every little thing, especially if one owned many horses, one would be bankrupt in short order. But the question still remained, *why?*

Her liver autopsy was sent to Vetpath Lab in Oklahoma, and the report stated the hepatic necrosis was massive, and further reported most cases of severe hepatic necrosis have a toxin or infectious cause. *Toxin?* She definitely had been exposed to toxins when she had been with her first trainer. Some horses cannot withstand the poisoning of their bodies with the soring applied to their legs. Many horses survive and seem to have no health problems. There are still some aged—over 15 years old—Walking Horses that are padded and sored still in the show ring. Many do not make it that long, either because they become lame, hateful, or can't get the blue ribbons any longer. Although it is not talked about, some die. Cookie was a young and small horse, and according to reports and the knowledge about that particular trainer, her soring applications had not been judicious.

Dr. Brandt and I talked at length about the definite probability Cookie had been poisoned in this fashion. The liver is a magnificent organ; it filters all the blood, cleansing the body of toxins, but when it is overcome, it will fail. He kept a sample of her liver for a long time, but in the end neither he nor I could figure out a way to prove soring methods had caused her death. He was more than willing to try to help me; I had never seen a veterinarian so angry. To think men were willfully causing not only pain, but illness and death in this manner insulted his training and dedication to healing legitimately sick horses. It insulted me too.

CHAPTER THIRTY-FOUR

My Gal Sunday

It was eleven o'clock in the evening and time to call it a day. First I needed to make a trip to the barn. Black Cashmier was due to foal and I wanted to be there to help if anything went wrong.

Different mares signal the coming birth of their foal with varied signs. Usually the udder fills with milk and little droplets of a waxy honey-colored substance that isn't yet milk form on the end of the teat. Occasionally milk will actually stream down the mare's hind legs, which isn't good because it wastes precious colostrum. Some mares give absolutely no signal birth is imminent. Cashmier had bagged up and her teats had shown the tell-tale sign of "waxing," a fairly sure sign birth would occur within a few days. Good horsemen keep close watch on their mares. It is difficult to figure out when a mare will foal, and a mare cannot be in a troubled labor very long before experiencing a bad outcome for one or both. Before the days of my horse foaling alarm, I was doing it the old fashioned way with many trips to the barn.

Cashmier was bedded deep in straw in the 20 foot by 12 foot foaling stall in the brand new wing of the barn. This was Hallelujah's barn. Mares to be bred, mares to foal and mares in residence made up the population— along with him, of course. It had been one of my later-in-life dreams and Cashmier was the first mare to deliver her baby here. My first peek at the soon-to-be momma showed nothing out of the ordinary. She was quietly munching her hay. Her eyes were soft as she walked over to me for a pat. All was well.

I set my alarm for 1 a.m. and went to sleep. I slept very soundly the first part of the night, and being startled awake by the alarm wasn't pleasant. Drowsily I pulled on my jeans, tucked in my short nightdress, donned a sweatshirt over it and went downstairs to find my boots. Before the purchase of a foaling monitor, these nighttime jaunts to the barn were necessary, but certainly not something I looked forward to.

It was dark outside, but fairly warm for the middle of April. I planned my foals to be born in warmer weather—no January birthing for me. I walked into the dark barn, but didn't turn on any lights; I used my flashlight instead. Because mares can control their birth time to some degree, and if they become agitated they could wait longer, I wanted to be as unobtrusive as possible. Again, she was calm, standing in the stall, very contented, and her hay gone. I quietly left.

Setting the alarm for 3 a.m., I crawled into bed. Checking a mare every two hours leaves a lot of room for error; if she was in trouble, two hours was too long to be of much assistance. One hoped and prayed to hit the timing just right. Following the same procedure as before, I looked in on Cashmier at 3. This time she seemed more awake, but it was as if she wanted her breakfast and was hopeful that was the reason for my visit. I looked at her and grumbled that I'd see her at 6 when I normally fed them; I just knew she wasn't going to have it this night, and I was really tired.

Sunday morning came and I went to the barn to feed. I was so sure the mare would keep her foal inside her another day, I didn't hurry to her stall to look, just fed as usual. Her stall was at the very end, so it was the last I came to. Opening the door, I was stunned to see a large white birth sack behind the mare which looked like a tee pee, with the top pointing up higher than the body. The foal! This was bad, really bad. Rushing through the stall door, I tore open the birth sack so the foal could breathe and hoped with all my heart I wasn't too late and that the foal hadn't been deprived of sufficient oxygen for too long.

The wet and glistening foal shook a bit as I released the sack, wiggled, and took a breath. It was lying with its head up, not flat out on the stall floor as they are when first pushed out of the birth canal. The foal had obviously been born very soon after I entered the barn, and it had been strong enough to try to escape the smothering birth sack, but without success. This sack was very tough; I actually had a slight problem ripping it open with my hands. There is no doubt in my mind the foal would have suffocated if I hadn't been there at exactly that minute.

Getting out of the birth sack encasing the fetus within the womb is one of several things that can go wrong at foaling. Many a horseman has found a beautiful, perfect baby still contained in its covering and very dead. Most of the time the sack rips as the birthing process goes along, or the foal breaks it as it struggles to get up. A mare seldom is helpful; she is tired and usually lies still to rest while the foal struggles to break free and gain its feet.

This foal was a black filly with long legs; her rear legs had all the crooks and bends that make a great Walking Horse. I was ecstatic. Cashmier's first great colt, Final Praise, had been put down because of a fatal illness; Odyssey, her second stud colt, was a terror. Cashmier was my dream brood mare, but I was having quite a time getting the offspring I wanted. Here was a really great prospect and, by a miracle, she was alive and well.

Sunday Praise was a princess among foals. She knew she was royalty and acted every inch the prima donna. She was one of three foals born very close together that spring; this had been the only time in my breeding history I bred three mares at the same time. The other two were stud colts. While they acted like boys, tearing around the pasture, bucking, snorting and picking on each other, Sunday stayed out of the fray in her blue foal blanket. I was going to show her in the weanling classes during the summer horse shows as I had shown both Final Praise and Odyssey. She was even prettier and had better conformation than either of them, and Final had won almost every class I showed him in. Yes, I had big dreams.

With those plans in mind, I body clipped her with big electric clippers. Baby hair can take nearly all summer to shed off the foals in varying places not all at once, and without clipping they look like moth-eaten creatures. The first show was in June, so I clipped her at 4 weeks of age. By show time, her hair would have grown back and she would have a smooth, dark black coat. Losing all that hair could make her chilled when I turned her outside, so she was dressed in a royal blue foal sheet. Her one less-than-perfect body part was her ears. Sunday had longer ears like her mom, not the shorter more refined ears of her sire. With her kind, big eyes and lovely long legs, I could overlook it, and I hoped the judges would.

Cashmier had been shown with her other foals, always placing very well. Classes included Weanling Class for the foal, Broodmare Class for the mother as well as the Mare and Foal Class for both to be shown together. We usually won those whenever we entered them. While Cashmier was already a professional show mare, Sunday would be taught to walk alongside her handler with as big a stride as her legs would allow. The babies had to be well behaved, which is no small trick as most dislike being removed from their mothers. The judge would judge them down for whinnying, balking, rearing—and sometimes flipping over—or trying to return to their moms. If they were acting up, they couldn't be seen to their best advantage; thus, Sunday had to learn to leave both Cashmier and the barn and go to work.

Sometimes Michal, who got the task of showing the foals, would take her on a walk much like a dog, along the bridle paths and down the driveway. Still, it was no guarantee she would be a good girl in the midst of strange babies and in a new place with mares and foals screaming to each other.

Her other lesson was to learn to pose, like dogs at the dog shows. This was to show body conformation, grooming, beauty and manners. The front feet were to stay side by side with the rear ones stretched out behind, also side by side; the head and neck must be up with the foal looking alert, ears forward—and stand still while the judge walked around her checking all sides. Sunday's brother, Final, had been a superb show colt. He seemed to love showing off and puffed himself up with importance.

Our first show was in June in Mason, Michigan. It was one of our bigger shows and a lot of foals would be competing. Both Sunday and her mother were groomed spotlessly, shined to perfection, with the customary ribbons (my favorite color—blue) fastened in their manes and forelocks. Their hooves were polished with special black hoof polish. They were beauties.

As Michal led Sunday into the indoor arena, Sunday seemed to have her mind on other things—the spectators in the bleachers, other horses, and center ring with the flowers and chairs for the judge and helpers—it all gave her something to gawk at. Her wonderful long-legged stride shortened as she refused to pay attention. I hoped when they lined up the judge would see her beauty, but walking around was a large part of the judge's score.

Unfortunately she wouldn't pay attention in the line-up either— wouldn't pose or stand still. I don't remember what placing we got, but it was definitely not the blue. Our next show was in July in Indiana, and I hoped for better behavior and maybe a first place ribbon.

This show offered the mare and foal class and the open weanling class as well as the futurity (a special added money class). Sunday would have three opportunities to show. Surely she would be better here. This show was outside; there were more flies and the sun was hotter, but the crowd noise was much less.

I held my breath as the judge walked around the other babies, checking all sides, front and back. Sunday was standing still and posing perfectly. "Oh," I thought, hardly breathing, "if she will only *stay* that way until the judge has looked at her!"

Michal glanced at me and I gave her a weak smile and crossed my fingers. The judge was getting closer–only one more weanling to go. He turned around to look at Sunday and I couldn't believe my eyes. She put her ears back and if she could, she probably would have spit at him. She started moving around, backed up, and wouldn't pose again with her feet together. *Oh brother.*

The next class wasn't better, and in that one she had her dam, Cashmier, standing beside her. Cashmier was like a rock, never moving a foot and keeping her head still and looking forward. Sunday, on the other hand, did the same thing as before. She waited until the judge was starting to look at her and sabotaged her class again. There was one more class to go and we almost scratched her, but hoped "The third time's the charm." But it wasn't. Because she was such a great individual, she got decent ribbons even with acting awful, but it was no fun for Michal or me. That was her last competition as a baby. The next year she would be a year old, a yearling. There were halter classes for that age group also, but we had learned our lesson. If she hated it that much, what was the use?

Sunday had an attitude in everything she did. If she liked it, she cooperated; if not, then we had a struggle on our hands, but I told myself and anyone else who would listen, "You know it takes 'attitude' to make a great show horse. All I have to do is channel it in the right direction." And hoped that I could.

When she was almost two years old, I advertised her for sale. My thoughts echoed what I've heard many times from other breeders, "I have the factory (meaning the sire and dam); I will breed more." After all, I was in the horse breeding business and I couldn't keep them all. Part of me, however, knew the factory theory was not entirely true. Full brother and sister horses are not all created equal. This is proven in the race horse world as well as in mine. Cashmier and Hallelujah had five horse progeny together that lived, and they were all different. Sunday was the best of all. There certainly was no guarantee that I could have reproduced Sunday, let alone one better.

A lady from California answered my ad about Sunday. I sent her a video, but she decided not to buy her. Later that summer a couple of sisters who showed with us, became interested in buying her. This time I was sure she was sold. They were nice young women and I felt Sunday would have a good home with them. Their trainer talked them out of buying her—it turned out he had another horse he wanted them to buy. Sunday remained mine. It seemed this mare was meant to be for me, so I decided to keep her and get her started under saddle. I wasn't really knowledgeable about *starting* a good show horse, therefore I sent her to Ralph, who had trained her sire, Hallelujah. I was excited. Without a doubt this was going to be a great endeavor.

A couple weeks went by and I was surprised Ralph hadn't called to give me rave reviews about Sunday. So I called him. "How's my girl doing?"

There was a slight hesitation on the line and then he told me, "She's a bitch."

Now the big pause was on my end. "How so?" I asked.

"She tried to kick me the other day." And he had more to say about her that was far from pleasant.

I had never seen anything like that from her, so I was surprised. We talked a little more and I never did hear any great and glowing words about my mare. I hung up more than a little disappointed.

Succeeding calls did not elicit any more great news. Pat, one of my boarders and a close friend, was going down to visit and when she came home I asked about Sunday.

"Ralph says she can 'walk a hole in the ground'," Pat told me. Say what? How come I didn't hear that? All I heard were negative comments. After a month, I told him I was bringing her home. Sunday was a pill to put it kindly, and even Ralph didn't want to get along with her, no matter how much talent she had. She was a character. She had some mulish tendencies and she was bossy as well. She couldn't be forced to do her best; she had to think working well was her idea, and you had to like her for herself. She and a trainer with preconceived ideas of horse behavior weren't going to get along. So she came home, and we soon became the Plantation Amateur Owned and Trained combination to beat.

In halter classes Sunday was a flop because she didn't want to do it–plain and simple. Under saddle as a pleasure show-horse she was suburb and knew it. At her first show as a two-year-old, she won all her classes and the judge told me after the show she was the best horse on the grounds–not just the best two-year-old, but best horse! He continued to be one of her staunchest admirers whenever he judged her.

Sunday was nine years old when I retired from showing, and again I thought I might sell her. She was too talented to simply go for short rides on a trail, or stand in the pasture getting fat. I called Diane, a lady who had previously shown interest in her during another weak moment when I thought about retiring from showing. I had cold feet that time and told her I couldn't sell Sunday. Diane would have taken great care of Sunday and said she would keep her until she died, but she couldn't buy her at the moment as she had too many horses of her own. Reason prevailed and I again realized that I couldn't part with Sunday even if it meant she would get fat, sassy and lazy, standing around the farm.

From her near disastrous birth to every possible sale being foiled, plus her survival from a mysterious horse sickness other horses succumbed to, Sunday had been saved for me. She was an opinionated and sometimes obstinate and bossy mare, but—she was my gal Sunday.

Sara and Sunday
Photo by Brian Richman

CHAPTER THIRTY-FIVE

Heartbreak

The sickness and untimely death of Cookie, probably caused by the inhumane training custom of soring, was the first horse related heartbreak. Another followed in the spring.

Black Cashmier, my charming black momma horse, was due to foal another Praise Hallelujah baby. Their cross was producing exceptional offspring. Final Praise had died, but Sunday and Bouquet of Praise, the next fillies, were promising show mares. I looked forward to this next birth.

Momma wasn't due yet, but every morning at feeding time I peeked in her stall to give her a special look and a pat on the neck. This particular early spring morning things were amiss. Cashmier stood in the corner of her stall with her head hanging down and her ears drooping. "What the heck?" I murmured.

Looking closer I saw a little black lump in the corner. It was the foal Cashmier had aborted. That was bad enough, but something was also wrong with the mare. I wasted no time calling the vet. Cashmier was current on all her horse shots including the one to prevent miscarriages, so this was another unwelcome mystery. Because of my mind to mind conversations with the animals through Mary Long, I knew animals grieved. I needed to give Black Cashmier and myself some closure after this devastating event. I named the little fellow Cashmier's Black Beauty, and Bob respectfully buried him in the woods. My heart ached both for Cashmier and myself. On the positive side of things, Bouquet of Praise, Cashmier's second filly born two years earlier, was fulfilling all my expectations.

Bo, as she was called, was very long legged and elegant. The morning of her birth my fence man had been building more rugged fences for the horses to begin tearing down (their favorite pastime it seemed). He happened to be walking by the foaling stall as I was trying to help Bo to stand. It was impossible. She was so tall and her long legs went every which way but straight down. She struggled to stand, all but knocking me over. I elicited Dave's help to pick her up. Finally she got the hang of it and was soon searching for mom's milk factory. Bouquet was a sweet foal, very unlike her sister Sunday, who was talented but opinionated. I was elated. She had every appearance of making a spectacular show horse.

Erica had entered our lives the spring before Bo's birth and the two of them became inseparable. She showed the weaning filly in halter classes and the next year in the yearling halter classes. They were hard to beat. Bouquet's long legged stride and her statuesque black beauty were destined for many blue ribbons.

The same year we lost little Cashmier's Black Beauty, Erica and I started two-year-old Bo under saddle. Her first show was in June and her second in July. She did well, no blue ribbons, but her performances were respectable; Erica and I were pleased with her progress and looked forward to bigger and better things. Sometime toward the middle of August when I went to feed the horses, I noticed Bo wasn't quite herself—not really sick, but sort of listless. She ate, but not with great gusto. I took a watch and wait attitude. The next morning she wasn't any better, but not worse. When I called the vet, he asked if she had any diarrhea and I answered "Not really."

Actually her bowels were slightly loose, but sometimes by eating grass, that happens. He gave her some medicine, but she still wasn't right. Four days later she stopped eating. Loading her into the trailer, we drove the hour to Dr. Brandt's clinic in Niles, Michigan. He started her on fluids and more medicine. Things did not look good for my lovely Bouquet. The next night before I was in bed, Dr. Brandt called and said I should have her put to sleep. Wiping away my tears, I told him to go ahead.

The next day another great young show mare on my farm, sired by Praise Hallelujah but owned by another lady, went off her feed. When I dumped in her grain and she didn't even look at it, I knew we had a problem. Wasting no more time, the mare was loaded in the trailer and rushed to Dr. Brandt's. By now anyone who was around any of the horses in any capacity looked for diarrhea and lack of appetite.

For sure, this mare had gotten to the clinic much sooner than my much loved Bouquet. If I had only known about the loose stools, if she had seemed sicker, if I had not waited, if, if, if. Unfortunately, the outcome for this horse was no better. Dr. Brandt said although she was responding to the treatment for her illness, she had developed serious laminitis in all four feet, was in extreme pain and should be euthanized. Everyone involved was agonized. Laminitis is a horseman's nightmare. It had caused the death of the great Secretariat in his retirement years and later the noble and much loved Barbaro after his horrendous Preakness accident.

Next, another boarder's horse showed signs of no appetite and diarrhea. She didn't wish to have the horse sent to the clinic as it was expensive and opted for the farm vet to treat him. Much money, time and vet calls later, the horse recovered. Then another one right on the heels of the previous gelding got sick. The same treatment was given and again the horse survived. Two more horses followed with sickness and recovery. For some reason each succeeding case seemed to recover faster and it wasn't because we found it sooner. It was a mystery. What in the world was this illness?

Somewhere in the middle of horses getting the illness, Sunday Praise, my most special mare, refused her morning meal. This was heart stopping for me. I had lost Bouquet and, although not mine, another of Hallelujah's great young show mares. *Oh, God*, I prayed, *not Sunday too!*

By now fear was my constant companion. What next? As the vet had done with all the other horses, I gave Sunday a shot of Banamine (a fever and pain reducer) and we raced to Dr. Brandt's clinic once again. When I unloaded her from the trailer, she charged toward the few blades of grass that were growing along the side of his driveway. I laughed delightedly at her bad manners. Dr. Brandt took her temperature and it was normal. It had already dropped several degrees from the morning. She seemed perfectly healthy, but I left her there for observation. The next day he called and told me to come get my mare. Sunday had been spared.

Blood samples were taken from the horses and sent away to Purdue. They came back negative for anything known, but were "Potomac Fever-like." All our horses were vaccinated religiously twice each year for Potomac Fever even though the vaccine is not known for great efficacy. The hope is it would at least lighten some of the symptoms and aid in recovery. Why some of these horses died, some recovered fast and some slowly, shall remain a mystery.

By now my nerves were pretty well shot. The barn, my refuge for peace and personal place of solace as I waited out my daughter's cancer, had become, itself, a place of sadness. I blamed myself, although no one knew what I could have done to prevent the disaster. Unfortunately, the year had yet another heartbreak for me.

That fall Nugget delivered a heart damaged foal that was euthanized after living only a few hours. After this episode I was fairly numb and I seriously wondered if I could take any more. Tears came easily and copiously. I thought about selling all my animals and closing the boarding barn.

CHAPTER THIRTY-SIX

Redeemed With Praise

B ack in the summer of 1996, a horse friend called to tell me she had recently bought a direct daughter of the great Pride of Midnight at the Shipshewana horse auction. She said the mare had been in pathetic condition and after a month she looked a little better but was still pretty thin. She was one of the last crop by Pride of Midnight. This was an exciting find, and here in my own back yard at that. I rushed over and quickly bought the mare. I continued feeding her generous amounts of good feed and vitamin and mineral supplements. My goal was to breed her to Praise Hallelujah. Genetically, the idea was sound. However, wanting to breed the old mare was easier said than done. It took until the next spring, but finally the vet pronounced her in foal.

The mare, Pride's Bittersweet, or Queen, continued to fatten up on the rich summer grass and her supplemental grain. Her hair became glossy and beautiful dapples appeared on her chestnut coat. Queen had a sweet disposition; even though apparently half starved in the past, she was a lady at feeding time and didn't push or shove the human handlers or other horses.

The following year on a warm May evening, Queen went into labor. I was there watching as unobtrusively as possible, but I was a little concerned. She was the first mare I'd watched that was up and down, up and down after the water broke and it worried me. I wondered if the foal was causing her discomfort. Perhaps it was positioned wrong. I called the vet, but would be at least half an hour before he would reach the farm. Eventually Queen lay down and started pushing. Thankfully, the foal was coming out in the proper position—no feet were bent inside the mare, and the front, not the rear feet were seen coming first.

When the foal was out of the mare, I quickly wiped his nose and mouth, but there was no movement, no struggling to raise his little wet head, indeed, no breathing, but there *was* a heartbeat—I could feel it fluttering under his ribs. I pushed on his sides and blew in his nostrils to give him artificial respiration. It was probably seconds, but seemed much longer, before he began to take short and then longer breaths. Now he was alive but unconscious. This was a first. I had never seen anything like it.

Thankfully, since I had called the vet earlier, he arrived right on time for the stressed foal. Dr. Caywood administered some drugs directly into the foal's jugular vein and the baby stirred, and then raised his head. As he struggled trying to get to his feet, I was impressed with how strong he was. Not wanting to take the chance that his first meal might be delayed any longer, the vet milked the mare.

"Boy," I said to the vet, "you do that so easily. I've tried it and can't get the milk out."

I was an expert cow milker, but their teats are long enough to fit into your hand. A mare's teats are tiny in comparison.

"We raised Percheron draft horses on my childhood farm, and sometimes we needed to milk the mares for the foal. I got really good at it." he explained.

He proceeded to put a small soft plastic tube through the foal's nose into his throat and down into his stomach. Next he poured the mare's colostrum, rich in needed nutrients, down the tube. The foal objected strongly to this procedure and began trying harder to rise. By now Bob arrived in response to my phone call, and he held the still wet and slippery foal securely. In a matter of minutes after that first meal, the colt was on his feet, searching for more of that warm white liquid.

Because for all intents and purposes the foal had been nearly dead, Redeemed with Praise seemed a fitting name for the light chestnut colt with the strikingly beautiful white mane and tail. As a weanling, he was spectacular. He moved with grace and style on his long legs, and his Tennessee Walking Horse gait was impressive. He had just the right looseness in his walk that meant as he grew older he would have a coveted ground-covering smooth stride. I was elated. He would be one of my prize colts to show, ride and maybe sell someday at top dollar.

God had different plans for Redeemed and they were nothing like mine. Our family learned Divine Plans do not always track with ours. Sharon's diagnosis of breast cancer only seven months earlier was certainly one example.

It became increasingly apparent that the lack of nutrition in the old mare was causing problems for the youngster. At about a year old he began growing funky and no amount of nutritional supplements made a difference. He was long legged, but very narrow and developed big bony humps on his croup and withers. He seemed to have no muscle, but was healthy and happy. I didn't have the heart to put him down–I mean, surely there was a reason I was there at his birth and saved his life–and there was no way I could ever sell him or give him away. I was responsible for him.

One day when Redeemed was about a year old, my husband brought one of his patients and his young teenage daughter out to the barn. The dad said he wanted to buy Sara a horse to keep her interested in school and doing well in her studies. That sounded like a wonderful idea for having a horse, but I didn't have anything available, only Redeemed and he wasn't saleable.

We talked about the situation as Sara petted Redeemed, her eyes alight with new found love. Redeemed nuzzled her arm in return. It looked like a friendship made in Heaven so we came up with a plan. If Sara would come out to the barn after school and help with chores, she could have Redeemed, but he could never leave the farm. The young horse had to be where I could keep my eye on him. Sara broke the gentle colt all by herself. Redeemed had a natural ground-covering gait and became a calm trail horse. If that was all there was to the story, it would be a good one, but Redeemed did more for Sara than just become her special horse.

Sara came from a depressed section of the city where domestic disturbance calls to the police department were commonplace and known drug areas were only houses away. I knew from that first look she gave to him that Redeemed had a special place in her heart, but I didn't know until later how much her having him to love and confide in helped save her.

She called him Mister and, after we'd known each other for some time and she'd slowly opened up to me at least a bit, she told me many evenings she would cry while she told him all her problems, including those caused by the peer pressure she was up against to become like her environment.

During her years at New Acre Farm, Sara became quite an accomplished rider. We were into showing the Walking Horses quite heavily at that time, and since all my own children had grown up, Sara was nominated to be our juvenile show rider. She graduated from high school and got a job, fulfilling her dad's desire. Sara gave Mister a lot of credit for keeping her on the path to better herself.

When Sara graduated from high school and left for her new work commitments, Redeemed found himself without a job and without someone to love. I put an ad in the local newspaper advertising two horses available for lease. One was Redeemed and the other was Rocky, an older horse. One afternoon a mom and her eleven-year-old daughter came to the farm. We discussed both horses and Redeemed's strange-looking body. Shelby chose Redeemed and a two-way rescue was on its way.

They were a good fit as Shelby had done some riding but was a little unsure of herself. With Redeemed to love and ride anytime she wished, she blossomed in more ways than just becoming a better rider. Like Sara, she also had peer problems in school. The girls were in a clique and treated her as an outcast, but she told me the boys were the meanest and belittled her love for horses, destroying some of her horse art. Understandably, she had times of depression and extreme loneliness. During the summer she was a constant figure at the farm, grooming, riding, or just sitting with Redeemed in his stall or pasture.

Shelby and Redeemed

I went out one morning to feed and saw a decorated paper tacked to his stall door: "Mister, I love you and I wanna say thanks for giving me my life back and most importantly making me happy. So thanks, thank you Mister."

That was one side of Mister's story. The flip side was the struggle Redeemed had with his strange body. When Sara trained him, he was quite agile. He didn't trip when he was ridden, and he could lie down and get back up. When he was four years old, he started getting stuck in the down position. Redeemed had a long narrow body with long legs. Because of the narrowness, he was pancake flat when lying down and when he did, for some reason he always lay flat, not up on his chest with his legs tucked under his body as most horses. He had little muscle mass and was like a beached whale when he got down.

He seemed to realize he was in a precarious position when down, so for days he slept standing up. Horses do this to a large extent. Nature has endowed them with locking joints in their legs that allow horses to sleep in this fashion. Usually after four days, Redeemed would give up and lie down. Our stalls are ten by twelve feet, but I had a larger foaling stall I could use for Redeemed that was double the length. However, it was soon apparent that it didn't matter what size stall Redeemed was in, he still got stuck.

Bob did the night time barn checks around nine. He checked Redeemed to see if he was standing, and he usually was up at that hour. If he wasn't, Bob would get him up, figuring a short rest was better than being stuck down all night. He most often lay down after Bob left. Later when he tried to get up, he flailed his long legs about, spinning around on his prominent hip bone. It didn't matter how deeply he was bedded in shavings on the rubber stall mat, the bedding got stuffed under his belly like a chock. Now he was totally blocked from getting up or moving.

Each morning the first thing I did was go to Redeemed's stall and see if he was up or down. In his younger years I could get him up by myself. If he hadn't jammed his head under his water bucket, or got it scrunched in a corner requiring Bob's help, I could put a lead rope on his halter and pull his head in the direction his long legs were lying on the ground. If he could raise his head off the ground with my pulling for all I was worth, he and I could get his center of gravity shifted enough that he could give a huge lurch and rise. As soon as he began to rise, I would drop the lead rope and back toward the empty corner. One day, he began to rise and then toppled over again—in my direction! I flattened myself into the corner, just avoiding a thousand pounds of horseflesh squashing me. Clearly this was not a safe method any longer, but some days I felt I had little alternative.

Everyone in the barn, boarders, stall cleaners and even Bob walking the dogs, all knew to look in the pasture for Redeemed and be sure he was still standing. In spite of his affliction, he seemed to feel good and ran with the other horses, although I wished he would not. If there was snow or mud on the ground, we could count on Redeemed slipping and falling down. A couple times I watched him run, slip, and fall and get right back up. I think it had to do with the first try. If somehow he managed it before he wore himself out spinning around and digging himself into a hole, he was up. Otherwise I would get the phone call, "Redeemed is down."

I tried to protect his hip bones by having Redeemed wear a horse blanket. This was also a problem because the blanket strap across his chest which kept the blanket on, prevented him from getting up even with help, necessitating blanket removal.

Even with using the horse blankets for protection as well as warmth because he had no fat either, he still got stall or pasture sores on his hips and shoulders. Depending on how long he was on the ground, the sore could be quite raw and painful. After much doctoring, they would heal in about a week, but without fail, as soon as he looked presentable, he went down and did it again.

The strangest thing was that he didn't stumble when ridden. I forbade the girls to run him while riding; I thought that would be too dangerous for horse and rider. He was seven years old in May and that summer he had a couple falls with Shelby. At first we all tried to overlook it, but having a horse fall while ridden is dangerous, even at a walk. His being stuck in the stall and pastures was also getting much worse.

For the previous two years I hadn't been able to get Redeemed on his feet by myself. Either he had worn himself out by the time I got there or had given up. I could pull on his lead rope and his head just came off the ground a few inches and then he let it fall back down. Sometimes I yelled at him; sometimes I cried in frustration. I just knew I could get him up if he would only try. But his try was gone.

I had to start enlisting Bob's aid. I pulled his head up, and Bob got behind his neck and pushed the horse's shoulders until Bob's face got red and the blood vessels stuck out. I hoped he wouldn't get a hernia. This worked each time, but I worried some day it wouldn't be enough. Then there was the day Bob had to take down a twelve-by-eight foot solid wood section of stall partition because Redeemed had gotten himself stuck so close to the wall there was no room to pull or push him. The situation was starting to look grim.

CHAPTER THIRTY-SEVEN

I Am Not There

Through all the ups and downs of Sharon's illness and the loss of my horses, finally some momentous and exhilarating news: Chessa was pregnant! Hal and I had waited for many years to have grandchildren. Erica, who had shared my life and love of the horses for years, was actually the correct age to have been a granddaughter if Sharon had had children. As our lives meshed together with the horses, I thought of Erica as a granddaughter, more than once. Chessa was our youngest, ten years younger than Sharon, and the only one of our four children who planned a family. Now we would have a grandchild of our own. Hal and I were excited and looked forward to October 2002.

On October 27, baby girl Haley Rose was born—but took not one breath of this world. We were all dumbfounded. How could this be? Chessa was healthy; she never smoked, drank, did drugs or even had drugs to deliver her daughter. But this granddaughter was not to be.

Yes, adversity comes. Animals die. Family members can get sick and die. I knew all that. But these things usually happened over a lifetime. I'd gone through it all in five years from Sharon's diagnosis of a particularly insidious type of breast cancer to the death of our first grandchild. The grief tore at my heart; sadness shadowed every hour, and my biggest question was, *Why?*

I remember standing in the barn aisle with my sister's youngest daughter, another special young person who shared my love of horses. Gabriella was going to Purdue School of Veterinarian Medicine at the time and was home on vacation. I broke down in big racking sobs. She put her young arms around me as I said, "I think I am having a breakdown."

"That's all right," she said soothingly, "you are entitled." That was all I needed to hear. It was vindication for my grief, sorrow and anguish. Forget medication, counseling and more internal torment. It was okay to feel bad. With those youthful empathizing words I felt my grief spill out and my healing begin. Sharon had been right. Sometimes all one needs is another to share your tears.

The world kept turning, the days coming and going and with it one of the happy horse and human relationships that had lasted seven years was slowly coming to a sad end. Redeemed continued to have more and more episodes showing his body condition was worsening. The practical side of me said to put him down. I kept receiving the thought and feeling from Redeemed that he wasn't ready, so as bad as the situation was, I kept getting him up and doctoring the many sores that got even worse. Of course, the problem was compounded by the fact that thirteen-year-old Shelby loved him and the fact he was only seven. He had never been sick or even lame a day in his life. I was the person who had to decide "when enough was enough"—and I was at a loss for what to do. I hated playing God.

I talked to Shelby about his worsening condition, and she realized that his stumbling and falling while she rode him wasn't a good thing, and his getting stuck was getting worse. Yet, she didn't want to think the end was nearing. In her youthfulness she was still optimistic, but I was not. I felt tired to the bone worrying about this special horse. I called my animal communicator friend, Mary, and talked with Redeemed. Sometimes the animals tell you when they are ready to leave the earth, or that they want to stay longer. Redeemed wasn't telling me much. Mary ended with, "You will know when it is time."

Finally one morning as Bob and I struggled to get him up, I knew in my heart the time had come. I told Shelby and she was upset. Her parents could see the adult side of things, but they were upset too, partly wondering how this would affect Shelby.

I called Sara, Redeemed's first young friend, and told her that if she wanted to say "Good-bye" to Redeemed she should come soon. I didn't see Sara when she visited, but I found a note the next morning. Sara was upset and a little angry with me. With Redeemed standing in his stall with his head over the gate, his eyes bright and looking at her intently, she couldn't fathom why I was putting him to sleep. Believe me, I understood her thoughts and feelings.

I suggested Shelby talk to Mary Long and Redeemed. Redeemed told Shelby he didn't want to leave her, but it was best we plan his departing so it could be peaceful and not because he was stuck somewhere and we couldn't get him up. He told her there were other horses in the barn she could love. He suggested Black Cashmier who was also without a job since she quit having babies. With everyone in sad agreement, I picked the day.

Shelby and Cashmere

Redeemed was a fooler. He looked weak and scrawny, but other than the fact his legs didn't always track right, and he couldn't get up on his feet, I knew he was strong. When the vet came to release him from his horse body, I warned him Redeemed was tough. Putting him to sleep wasn't going to be like putting down a sick horse.

The first injection makes them unconscious and they fall to the ground. The second, given while the horse is lying down, stops the heart. Redeemed had a big heart—in many ways—and it took a big dose to close this chapter of his exceptional life. Shelby later told me she felt his spirit around her for two days, and then he left to gallop his way to Heaven.

Shelby was a very artistic thirteen-year-old. She drew beautiful horse pictures and wrote exceptional stories and poems. She gave me the ballad she wrote about Redeemed as an English assignment, to share in *The Horse That Wouldn't Trot*.

Shelby told me this story about her ballad. "At the end of the school year we had a 'coffee house' where we drank hot chocolate, ate snacks and sat around the room on chairs, listening to poems by our peers and school staff. After a history teacher and the school police officer finished reading, I volunteered to read my ballad. I sat on the stool and read aloud my poem to the class. Keeping in mind that this class had plenty of guys and gang members, after I was done reading I heard all these sniffles. I saw the history teacher get up and get a Kleenex, since she was really crying..."

My Last Goodbye
I remember clearly, almost like it was yesterday
And I still mourn for him, even today
The times we shared, the love we had
Every moment together and how he made me so glad
Four months have passed, since that terrible day
When death took him from me, took Redeem away

I remember that cold night I stayed at the barn
With nothing but a sleeping bag to keep me warm
I stayed all through the night, there with him
If it hadn't been so cold I would have done it again

I spent every chance with him I could get
He was one special horse, one I will never forget

I even called Mary Long, an animal communicator
I still recall that three way conversation even though it's five
Months later

I remember the talks I had with his owner
The whole way we were in this together

I remember our last times we shared, a November Sunday
It was a beautiful afternoon, a gorgeous sunny day
I saddled up and headed out with every one of my friends

I can certainly say it was a great way to end
It was one of our best, that time on the trail ride
All too soon, I dismounted, and led Redeem inside
I gave him a good rubdown and put him in his stall
I sat down in there and wrote a poem for his door wall
I cried as I said my last words
Unlike him, he just stood as if taking in everything he heard
I told him how much I loved him, kissed him and took a last look
With one final glance I stepped outside as I shook

That was the last time I saw him, before they put him down
I'll always remember him when November 21st comes around

The Wednesday after I sat in Math class
I suddenly looked up as I felt his soul was released at last

I still have a lock of his hair hanging on my wall
And remember that poem I hung on his stall? It said:
A close friend of mine died today
As he went up to Heaven angels parted the way
Arms open, they welcomed him in
It was his time, but it hurt me within
Now I hear him say, "Do not stand at my grave and cry
I am not there I did not die."

Redeemed's shortened life and the loss of little Haley Rose begged the question: why do some have troubled short lives and some never have the chance at all? Why do healthy young women get cancer? I had to believe a Higher Power had control of our lives, both human and animal. We are here on earth for a purpose and perhaps we will die without knowing exactly what that purpose is, but as Shelby's ballad states: "Do not stand at my grave and cry, I am not there, I did not die."

CHAPTER THIRTY-EIGHT

Honey and Smokey

Justice Amen was Nugget's and Praise Hallelujah's second foal. The fact that Nugget's first foal, Gifted, had developed contracted tendons didn't worry me when I considered breeding Nugget again. I thought it had likely been a fluke.

Nugget's original owner, Connie, sold Nugget to me with the provision she would get the first foal, so I hadn't raised Gifted myself after she was weaned. Maybe the filly had not been fed properly, hadn't had enough exercise, or any number of possible scenarios. The veterinarian who had first treated her said to cut back on her food—actually starve her—the theory being that she was growing too fast, and feeding her less, especially less protein, would slow down the growth of the bones and allow the tendons to catch up. This didn't work for Gifted. She ended up with her ribs showing and she still had her problem legs.

My foal, Justice Amen, was born uneventfully. She was a sweet filly, the color of honey, so her barn name became Honey. We took her to some horse shows when she was three to five months old where Michal showed her in weanling classes for the baby horses. She did well and ended up High Point Weanling for one of our state organizations. As a baby she enjoyed her horse friends, ran around kicking up her heels, galloped from one end of the pasture to the other, ate lots of green pasture grass in the summer and the best hay I had in the winter. She received ample petting and brushing from her humans. She was a normal, contented youngster. Honey was one year old February 2 of 2001, when I began to notice her front legs looked too straight. We were about to embark upon a very sad journey.

A month later I talked with my farrier, the man who trimmed the horses' feet and nailed on their shoes. He said that he had noticed it too, and was concerned. He tried trimming her hooves differently. She had little movement or flexion in the ankle because the area between the ankle and foot, called the pastern was growing too straight. She wore the toes off her hooves which made the condition worse, as now she was standing almost straight up like on tip toes. He trimmed her heels lower to put stretch on the tendons and lower her foot. That didn't really help, so he tried putting a special shoe on so she couldn't continue to wear away the toe, but that didn't help either. We just could not get her pasterns to stretch down so she wasn't walking around on posts.

It was like watching an impending collision between two trains; I could see it coming but I couldn't find the switch to stop it. A call to the feed man gave us several feed options. We changed her grain, gave her a free choice mineral, hoping that if the problem was a mineral imbalance, she would eat what she needed to correct it. Horses have an innate knowledge of what they need and many times will choose the correct feed if it is available. In this case, however, the problem seemed to get worse. All of a sudden she had a growth spurt. Her legs which were already long and elegant grew even longer, but not in correct proportion. She looked like a filly on stilts.

Her front legs started to knuckle over at the ankle joints, and her left one was the worst. She had the same condition called contracted tendons Gifted had developed. The tendon down the back of her front legs from the knee to the ankle couldn't stretch or grow as fast as the bones were growing in her legs. The pull on the back of her front legs caused her ankles to buckle over. Strangely, the hind legs were normal.

In May I decided that no supplements, feed changes or foot care was going to help Honey. Surgery was finally suggested. In hindsight, I wish I had been advised about, and decided on, surgery earlier, but Honey was my first experience with contracted tendons, and she had a very bad case. By now she was fifteen months old.

The veterinarian performed a surgery called bilateral inferior and superior check ligament desmotomy, simply meaning that he surgically snipped the ligaments in the leg above and below the knees so they could stretch. He wasn't very encouraged about her condition. During the surgery he hadn't gotten the release he had hoped for, and after it she didn't straighten out as he had expected. What usually happens with this surgery is over time the ligament heals back, but with more length where it had been snipped; and the leg can perform normally, or at least close. It's not a complicated or unusual surgery, but Honey's legs were already quite bad. It assuaged my guilt somewhat when he said it probably wouldn't have made a big difference if I had brought her sooner; she seemed to have a bone growth problem as well which was making Honey's case harder.

She came home from the hospital all wrapped in thick bandages, with the instructions to give pain medication, keep her in a stall for two weeks, and rebandage two times a week. She could be hand walked two times a day but for only five minutes. After the two weeks, she could be turned out in a small pen for just minimal exercise—no running.

When we took the bandages off, there was no noticeable improvement in the way she stood. By August both ankles were knuckling over worse than before. She had a hard time walking, but it didn't seem to bother her. She took it in stride as though that was the way all horses walked. She didn't seem to be in pain; she just had grotesque looking legs and a stilted walk. Running was out of the question.

I was becoming embarrassed for anyone to see her. Our horses can hang their heads over their stall gates so they can look around and people can pet them. From that viewpoint, Honey looked just fine, but when she got visitor petting I sort of rushed them away before they could notice anything else. I think my horse friends were shaking their heads wondering why Honey was still among the living. I thought many times about putting her to sleep, but I couldn't–not yet. It didn't seem as if it was her time. My regular farm veterinarian, Dr. Hammond, felt sorry for both of us, but he couldn't offer any hope.

Honey was in a holding pattern. She had her pain medication and all the food she wanted. It didn't seem to make a difference what she was fed, she still got a little worse each week, but still I couldn't put her down. All the vibes I received from Honey were she wanted to stay on earth longer. If she'd been in obvious pain, it would be an easy choice; but she wasn't, and with her sweet temperament, she seemed content with life. Then other changes to my herd vied for my attention...

On a beautiful October morning, I went to the horse barn to feed as usual. The horses were pastured at night while it was cooler and kept inside the barn during the heat of the Indian summer days, enjoying their fans. All the animals were quiet, content, and devouring their grain quickly. Two hours later I returned to the barn. It was my quiet time of day, the time I had for myself with the horses. I got Magnolia, who was sired by The Wiseman, a famous Harlinsdale stud and was in foal to Praise Hallelujah, out of her stall for grooming. Magnolia was a special mare I had purchased specifically to mate with my stallion. I had great hopes for the offspring. She seemed a little agitated but not overwrought. I tied her up to groom her and noticed that her tummy was smaller. First-time mares usually don't get really big bellies like they do after they have had several foals, but I realized that hers looked odd.

My heart almost stopped as I realized that the reason for her strange behavior was she had foaled and left her baby out in the pasture! I got my friend Pat, who was at the barn visiting her own horse, to accompany me and we went looking for a dead baby. It made some sense that she would have left it if she knew it was dead. I couldn't imagine a mare leaving a live foal, coming in the barn and eating her breakfast as usual. Because the foal was a month premature, this was the likely scenario. I looked down the fence line of the pasture and kept walking. I had no idea where it might be, I just started walking. Near a corner I saw a dark form—the dead foal, I guessed. I slowed down, putting off what I expected to be a bad deal.

As I got much closer, I could see that the dark form was outside of Magnolia's pasture. She had either delivered the foal close to the fence and pushed it underneath and out on the other side, or in struggling to get up, the baby had rolled under the fence. Now I really was upset with myself that I hadn't noticed she was close to having the foal, and separated her from the other mares, keeping her safe in a small pen near the barn. I hadn't done it because she was a whole month away from delivery, had not bagged up, and her belly still didn't look greatly enlarged. I disliked distressing the mares by separating them from their friends too soon. But now I was playing the blame game.

When I got to the foal, I quickly knelt down beside it discouraged by this sad turn of events, and ran my hands over its sun warmed back. Under my hand I saw the foal's sides slowly going up and down. I stroked it, and the baby unhurriedly lifted its head and looked at me. My pulse raced as I turned around and yelled to Pat who was several strides behind me, "The foal is alive!" It was a boy, all dried off from the morning sun and pretty darned contented for a brand new "orphaned" baby. I grinned ear to ear. A rather major horse disaster had been adverted and I still had my dream foal. Smokey pretty much lived his life as he entered it; if he could, he would eat or sleep through any of life's problems.

I looked around the pasture area and saw a path worn in the dirt where Magnolia had run up and down the fence. Had she been trying to retrieve her baby? Or guard him from other horses? It defied logic that even a new mother would run off for the barn and leave her baby. I would never know why it happened, but right now I had to get him to the barn and his momma. He needed his mother's first milk, the colostrum, as soon as possible. I guided his front end and Pat pushed his little bottom to the barn, a rather tedious journey. Even though he was rather calm about it all, he wouldn't go in a straight line and wanted to stop. We finally arrived at Magnolia's stall door, opened it and shoved the colt inside. I wish I could say he just walked up to the milk bucket between Magnolia's hind legs and got his first meal, but that is not what happened. First of all, Magnolia took one look at him and said in no uncertain terms, "What *is* that?" Thank goodness, she was not aggressive or mean; she just didn't recognize or welcome this little stranger with open arms.

Magnolia kept moving every time Smokey got close to her hind legs. I could almost hear her say, "You want to do *what?*" We tried holding her and shoving Smokey's head to the udder, but he just sat on our arms. I remembered trying to help other foals drink their first time, and it always ended up with my being frustrated. The more you push, the more they resist. I was grateful that Magnolia in her maternal forgetfulness was not nasty; she was just ignorant, and a few hours later she remembered she was a mom and had a job to do.

Smokey had the usual first six weeks of his life, drinking milk and running with his mother in their private pasture. Although they were separate, they were beside the other horses; all was well. One evening when they came for supper, I noticed Magnolia was walking very slowly, and one of the people who had a horse boarded on the farm said she noticed Magnolia had been lying down in the pasture, an uncommon thing for a nursing mother. The mares usually stand guard while their foals sleep.

I checked her out; she didn't seem to have a stomach ache, but limped a little when I led her around. I couldn't find anything out of the ordinary requiring an emergency call to the vet. I thought I would call in the morning if she wasn't better.

In the morning, she was much lamer, making no sense at all. I thought she might have laminitis, a condition where their feet get incredibly sore usually because of overeating or an infection. The vet did not think it was laminitis. He was afraid it might be acute EPM.

EPM, or Equine Protozoal Myeloencephalitis, is a disease caused by a parasite which invades the nervous tissue of the horse, causing myelitis and/or encephalitis. It is not spread horse to horse, but rather through a host, the opossum. Parasite infected opossums' feces can contaminate pastures and hay. Symptoms are many times vague and varied. Magnolia fit the part of lameness, weakness, difficulty in moving, especially in getting up. The shocking thing to me was how fast her condition was deteriorating. Several years earlier I'd had a couple other boarded horses in the barn diagnosed with EPM. Their symptoms were also vague. One had difficulty swallowing, finally to the point his food got caught in his throat; the other was shockingly lame but nothing like Magnolia and both recovered after a long and expensive treatment.

On the second day she lay down and couldn't get up. We fed her where she lay, gave her water frequently and Smokey nursed from her. The treatment was an anti-Protozoal drug and anti-inflammatories, but it was like pouring them down a hole; they seemed to have absolutely no effect. She tried to rise, but fell back down. She was a large mare, and we were concerned she would fall on Smokey.

Each day Magnolia became weaker and thinner, but appeared in fairly good spirits. She didn't seem in pain; she just couldn't move. She ate well and produced milk which the foal suckled from her recumbent form. Smokey was eating some hay at this point, so he was doing all right. I knew she was not going to make it, but Dr. Hammond and I agreed that as long as she was reasonably happy and not suffering, and the longer she could feed Smokey, the better.

Six days after I noticed her illness, she took a big turn for the worse. It was late evening after our family had been out for the evening. I checked on her before going to bed. She didn't want to eat, not even the choicest pieces of hay. She also wouldn't drink anything and for the first time, I noticed she was in distress. Apparently the Protozoa had eaten away at her spinal cord to the point of pain.

I called the on-call vet and got him up from bed. He wasn't the one who had been treating her, but all the vets at the Weldy Clinic knew of her tragic condition. The one thing Magnolia had requested when I talked to Mary Long about her disease, was she not have a spinal tap. It is a painful procedure but the only one that definitively diagnoses EPM. I told her she wouldn't. Because her case was so severe, there was no real reason for it, and at any rate, she was already being treated aggressively for that illness. The vet gave the merciful injection and Magnolia passed quietly away. Because she was insured, the vet then did the spinal tap which would later positively diagnose her illness. Now I had a six-week-old foal to take care of and no mother.

We left Magnolia in the stall with Smokey for overnight. It was the first part of November, snowing and nasty. Poor Bob had the awful job of pulling her body out of the stall in the morning with the tractor, loading her up on a big truck, and taking her to Dr. Brandt who would perform the required autopsy and dispose of her body.

Smokey didn't exactly seem to miss his mother; he was pretty calm about losing her; but still, he was lonely. Raising an orphan foal by itself isn't the best thing. Sometimes another nursing mare can be found who will nurse a strange baby. I couldn't locate one, but at least, Smokey required a friend. Smokey had to now learn how to eat milk pellets made especially for orphan foals. The large foaling stall had a camera monitor feeding pictures to the television in my den, and I kept going back to it, looking to see if he was eating. He wasn't. I made many trips to the barn and asked anyone else out there to stop in and encourage him to eat by standing by the feed box and stroking him. That seemed to help, but if he was left alone, he wandered away. Eventually he started gobbling his pellets and I breathed a sigh of relief.

While this was going on, Honey was sending me thought signals. She would be the perfect little mare to foster the young orphan; she couldn't hurt him even if she wanted to, and she also needed a friend. She couldn't be with any other horse because her walking was so disabled, she barely hobbled. Bob put some two by fours across the width of the large foaling pen dividing it in half, but keeping the top low so Smokey could reach over and touch Honey. We hung a big bag full of hay right between them and as Honey ate, Smokey put his little nose in the bag with her. This was going to work out just fine.

It was the first part of November; Smokey was doing very well and Honey was so happy and content. She finally had found her calling. I was able to put them out together in a small area, but by the end of December, Honey was almost walking on the fronts of her ankles. The time had come to say good bye to her. Smokey would be fine now, he thought himself quite the little horse.

The morning the vet came, Honey was quiet and peaceful. I led her out to the inside arena under one of the overhead lights so the vet could easily find her jugular vein. Honey stood at attention, not moving around as is common in horses, with her ears pricked forward, just as pretty as she could make herself. When the vet administered the injection that would give her back her beautiful body in spirit, she gracefully collapsed on the ground. There really was no grieving at Honey's passing into a better world. Everyone in our barn was mindful of her courageous spirit and her loving care of little Smokey. We all gave her a much earned, *"Well done!"*

Recently a friend sent me this internet poem. I don't know where it originated, and couldn't find who the author was, so I can't give credit, but if it had been written for Honey and me, it couldn't have been any better:

THE GRANDEST FOAL
I'll lend you for a little while
My grandest foal, He said.
For you to love while she's alive
And mourn for when she's dead.

It may be one or twenty years,
Or days or months, you see.
But, will you, till I take her back
Take care of her for me?

She'll bring her charms to gladden you,
And should her stay be brief
You'll have treasured memories
As solace for your grief.

I cannot promise she will stay,
Since all from earth return.
But, there are lessons taught on earth
I want this foal to learn.

I've looked the wide world over
In my search for teachers true.
And from the throngs that crowd life's lanes
With trust I have selected you.

Now will you give her your total love?
Nor think the labor vain,
Nor hate Me when I come
To take her back again?

I know you'll give her tenderness
And love will bloom each day.
And for the happiness you've known
Forever grateful stay.

But should I come and call for her
Much sooner than you'd planned
You'll brave the bitter grief that comes
And someday you'll understand.

Honey and Smokey's deep but brief connection proved that it isn't the amount of time that counts, but the true quality of emotion, caring and love that is shared. That same principle of devotion came true several years later for Sharon, when an extraordinary young man helped her through her hardest days.

CHAPTER THIRTY-NINE

Retirement

Out of necessity, most domesticated stallions lead a life of solitude and varying degrees of loneliness. The vision many may have in their minds of a beautiful and powerful stallion running free with a band of mares is not the reality for most stud horses. Perhaps a very few have this option along with the stallions of the wild feral horse herds, but it is not the norm.

Praise Hallelujah was like most domesticated studs; he had a career. He was exhibited at horse shows so prospective mare owners could see his talents and desire his services, but he was kept away from the other horses for his protection as well as theirs. He was much too valuable to be injured by an irate mare in the pasture. In his case, his paddocks always were close to the pastures, but separated by a strip of vacant land and double fences. He could see but not get to the other horses.

This strategy worked very well as long as I was riding and training him on a regular basis. He participated in his last show when he was fifteen years old. It was a bittersweet year. One of the reasons I brought him back from his earlier retirement of only one year, was because I had lost two of his best daughters to illnesses, and I missed showing him. When you work with any animal on a regular basis, you develop a rapport that can become very deep. "Praise Hallelujah" and "Rose Miller" were almost synonymous. Mention one of those names and almost anyone with knowledge of Tennessee Walking Horses in that era would think of the other. Some people didn't want to see him back in competition. When a good horse retires, they heave a sigh of relief that now they do not have to contend or compete with him anymore. But he also had his loyal public followers who were glad to see him back.

He didn't seem to enjoy that last show year as much as he had before. He fretted more about our mares when they left the stabling area, going around and around in his stall, stirring up the bedding and on occasion getting himself into a sweat. As long as they were all in the stable area with him, he was content. They were *his* mares! He had brought them from home and he didn't want any other stallion looking at them. I knew what he was thinking without any help from Mary, my communicator friend. We showed all the horses we brought, but we never took Hallelujah out of his stall at the same time we did the mares—except once.

We had chosen a class for Nugget and then two classes later, one for Hallelujah. The horses had to go through inspection before their classes which meant they had to be in the same area at the same time. Nugget had been inspected and was in the warm up area beside the show arena waiting for her class with Michal, her rider. We tried to keep Hallelujah from seeing her, but his stallion senses were too much for us. I think he first smelled her and then spotted her. Various horses stood all around, including other stallions who might see his mare and that was "all she wrote." He started jumping around and calling to her. Sitting on his back, I was in jeopardy, no doubt about that. If I had been younger with more guts than sense, I might have toughed it out, but with his mind gone, his required show gait would be gone too. There was no sense in trying to exhibit him; I took him back to the barn.

At one other show close to home, stabling was set up in such a way Hallelujah couldn't see his mares. They were right beside him, but out of sight because of a solid partition. He went round and round in his stall. If I tied him up, he pawed a big hole in the dirt floor with a front foot and kicked the side of the stall with a back foot. This was not the same horse I had showed earlier in his career. I took him out of the stall and led him around the grounds in front of the stalls, so he could see his mares, who quietly blinked at him, wondering what the commotion had been about. He quieted down; yet putting him back in the stall, caused the same behavior to start up again. Fortunately, we were only one hour away from home, and I took him back. The proverbial writing was on the wall—permanent retirement was right around the corner.

My heart ached because I knew what would happen when he was totally retired. Praise Hallelujah would be promoted through his numerous show offspring, and they would carry the New Acre Farm banner now. That would leave little time to ride Hallelujah. He would still have mares to breed, and he would have his small grassy paddock to run in, but it would not be the same, and I knew he would change.

In between training the mares and my other house and farm chores, I tried to ride him on the trails just for fun, but it didn't turn out to be fun for either one of us. Hallelujah's mind wandered back to the barn and pastures and he seldom seemed to enjoy our outings.

Then one day, after Hallelujah had gone about half the length of our riding path along the creek bordered by lush tall trees, he suddenly put on the brakes and turned for home. In his stallion mind apparently that was as far as he wanted to go away from the mares in the pasture. I was annoyed, but I had to admit I was also intimidated. I didn't know *this* horse. This Hallelujah was not my show ring partner, the one I'd led to judges and ridden hard and gaited to victory after victory. This new horse flicked his head with willfulness and snorted his possessiveness about his mares that bordered on obsession. He was not the same as in years past; then again, neither was I. When you are in your sixties, any kind of activity that could get you thrown to the ground could result in dire consequences. Sadly, I let him head for home and used all my horse knowledge to insist he go home at a somewhat quiet and safe speed.

I didn't ride him a lot after that. He was very content to be ridden in the arenas, but I had to ride the mares in that area for training and wasn't very enthused to ride him there. He was always easy to breed, cooperative for anything you wanted to do with him on the ground, but I could sense him slipping away, becoming more *horse* than my companion. Of course, it was my fault. I let him morph into becoming just a horse. The stallion who whinnied when he saw me coming now whinnied only for the mares. We were drifting apart emotionally.

In earlier years I had mentioned to a horse acquaintance that life with Hallelujah was a little like my marriage to Hal. A lot of give and take working toward a common goal. In Hal's and my case, even though we were like ships passing in the night, not always spending a lot of time together, our relationship worked. Now Hallelujah and I had different goals. I had other horses to train, and he had his mares to worry about. I gave him the best of care, but not the closeness of my companionship, and our relationship was *not* working.

I asked Erica to start riding him for me to see if we could get him going on trail rides again. Because she was in her twenties, she was definitely more suited to the venture, and she had no fear. Erica was a born horsewoman, however, we should have planned the endeavor a little better. She had a little problem in the same spot along the creek I had, but got him to continue on almost twice as far.

At the end of the creek trail is a little copse of woods that leads to another big field. She got to the end of the woods when Hallelujah decided that was far enough. This time he reared straight up on his hind feet and spun around. Erica's foot slipped out of one of the saddle stirrups, but she kept her seat on the horse. Next he started bucking, not like a rodeo horse, but enough to unseat a rider in a small English saddle. Erica decided to dismount before the horse unseated her. She led him back towards the barn a little ways to the old mounting block we have along the trail and got in the saddle again.

He was a little closer to the barn by now, but there was still no reasoning with him. She held the reins firmly in her hands and sat quietly being sure not to touch his quivering flanks with her heel, and managed to get him home "walking on his tip toes"—taking baby horse steps, all the while feeling like he could become airborne at any minute. Hallelujah's nostrils were dilated and he was snorting with every stride, his eyes bright with desire to return to his harem. In retrospect, it may have worked better if she had just taken him a little farther each time instead of going a much farther distance the first time. She followed that procedure later, and although she could trail ride him, my faith in him, and in my ability were shaken, and I didn't try it again.

That next January, on my birthday, I decided on the spur of the moment to go for a quick birthday ride on Hallelujah. He hadn't been ridden for a couple months, but I didn't anticipate any problem. I was just going to ride him in the inside arena. He seemed really happy to have the attention, loved being groomed and saddled. There were already two other ladies riding their horses in the arena, but that shouldn't present a problem either. I led him out to the arena, mounted and started to ride. He was frisky and he did a little buck jump, but nothing to unseat me. He was just exhibiting high spirits—strutting his stuff to impress the other two horses. His breath looked like spurts of fog in the chilled air, and I was enjoying the ride. He was a little too spirited to canter or lope, but that was fine. I just wanted a breath of the fresh, crisp, winter air and to enjoy my horse.

As we went around a corner, one of the barn cats sprang out into the arena, right under Hallelujah's feet. Cats have a warped sense of humor sometimes. This little episode was seen by one of the other riders and she stated emphatically there was no good reason for the cat to spring under the horse's feet. Naturally, Hallelujah jumped in the air and off to the side–a spook. I was still in the saddle when he came down although a little off to one side. Then the cat jumped again, this time probably because it was frightened at almost having a horse land on it, and my horse jumped again. The last jump popped me out of the saddle and onto the ground. Slam went the back of my head against the frozen ground! The arena is sand, but exactly where I was deposited had some water dumped on it and the earth had frozen.

Ever since I'd fallen off a horse in the woods a couple of years previously, I decided wearing a riding helmet was an excellent idea. Sure, you gave up the wind in your hair, got your hair all messed up and you got hot, but it was a good practice. I got to the point that not having it on my head made me feel naked, yet this day I didn't remember to put it on. I had been in such a hurry to grab a little riding enjoyment, I never thought about my helmet.

As the back of my head hit the dirt, I saw stars and heard things as if from miles away. I sensed that one of the girls had gotten Hallelujah, who far from being a terror to the others, had just ambled up to one of the horses where he was grabbed and led back to his stall. I slowly sat up and wished I hadn't; the barn was spinning. Long story short, I had a slight concussion and the rest of my body felt like it had been run over by the horse himself. It took weeks to recover, and I lost more of my nerve for riding horses, especially Hallelujah.

Hallelujah's outside paddock was approximately 50 feet by 200 feet. It was a nice run, and had a little grass which he kept grazed down to millimeters. He could see the other horses, but not get to them. I opened up his paddock into another pen, giving him more room, but at the same time taking him closer to the boarded horse pasture. Hallelujah's paddock was adjacent to the mare pasture, where I kept my own and those that came for breeding. Out of convenience, I kept a couple young geldings there also.

That did not sit well with him at all; he just wanted mares in his proximity. He hated the geldings and charged the fence and his stall door as they went past.

I had noticed that my other stallions also had a distinct dislike of geldings. At different times, two different stallions shared the breeding wing of the barn which housed the studs, the mares and the young horses. The stallions all seemed to respect each other. Hallelujah always wanted to go see the other stallion if I was leading him past his stall, but it was not with a look of hatred. It was more like, "How's it going, guy?" If I let him sniff the other stud's nose, there was squealing and snorting, but not a war. It was very strange to me. I finally came to the conclusion that Hallelujah knew the geldings were *Its* and in the wild there would be no place for them. He wanted to drive them off the farm if he could.

One day in the summer, the horses pushed down a fence between the boarded horses, which were mainly geldings, and my horses which were mostly mares. One particular gelding, Last Chance, thought he was the best thing that could possibly happen to a mare. He nickered to them, chewed lovingly on their necks and if they were in season, actually tried to service them. He chased the other geldings away from them, keeping his own little herd—and here he was—in the pasture right outside Hallelujah's paddock and in with *his* mares!

Hallelujah was beside himself with rage. The girls who did the evening chores didn't notice what had happened until it was feeding time when they saw the horses were mixed up and Chance was missing. Chance had quietly blended in with the mares and the girls didn't recognize him, but Hallelujah certainly did. By that time, my stallion was in a lather with steam coming off his hide and he was breathing heavily. I don't know how his fence held him. With less provocation from the other geldings, he rather routinely ran into his 2 inch by 6 inch board fence, breaking the boards or knocking them off the posts to display his ire. It took some time to cool both his senses and his overheated body.

One late afternoon in January, I got a phone call from Sarah, one of the girls who fed the horses in the afternoon. I answered and she said in a breathless voice, "Hallelujah is caught in the fence. I don't know how to get him out." I told her I'd get Bob, who fortunately for all the horse and cow happenings on the farm, had a business that he could run from the house.

After phoning Bob, I ran out the door and sprinted to the barn. It was a slow sprint because of a couple of horse-related knee injuries. Fence wire cutters are kept hanging in a special place just for these happenings. Horses are accident prone. If they can manage to get into trouble, they will. Many times they stick their front feet in the wire mesh field fence. Sometimes they can pull the foot out, sometimes they pull the fence apart, and sometimes they are stuck. Usually one can cut the wire, and pull the foot out; but sometimes it isn't very simple or easy.

I grabbed the cutters from the wall and Bob caught up with me on the way to the paddock. Going out the door I could see Hallelujah lying on his left side with both of his hind feet hung about three feet off the ground, causing quite a twist in his lower back. As I approached his head, he raised it off the ground a few inches, rolled his eyes up at me and nickered softly. He was in a mess and knew it. As I patted his head and pushed it back on the ground, Bob went to the back end with the cutters. Hallelujah's feet were through the fence about 6 inches and he was stretched tight; just cutting the wire might not get him out. Hallelujah would still need to pull his feet back through, and then get up.

Bob cut the hole and then I pulled gently on a rope attached to his halter, clucked to him and shut my eyes hoping for the best outcome. Hallelujah gave a lurch, the fence twanged, and I winced, but he made it to his feet and stood, holding one hind foot off the ground. A quick inspection showed no cuts, but the leg was swollen. We didn't think he had been there long. It was a mercy Sarah had come out early that day for feeding and found him.

He limped to the barn where we doctored the leg with cold water and liniment as well as giving him a shot of pain medication. Studs are tough. It seems they can prevail where others horses might not. In a few days, he was pretty much back to normal except for a big lump on his neck and a sore back.

Hallelujah was eighteen years old and at this point I was getting pretty darn tired of such behavior. He could have really hurt himself getting caught in the fence. Hallelujah was not a happy stallion. Other stallions in his position might be, but he was not. He and I were in a situation of our own making. I had stopped riding him and giving him the special attention he had grown to expect. Next, I had become afraid to ride him.

I told myself he wanted for nothing in the way of care, and he had a few mares to breed; he was earning his keep. He didn't have to be ridden, he was retired and he should enjoy life. But he had been showing me for the past year this was not the life he wanted. For that matter, what did *I* want? I had been on the fast track of breeding mares and showing horses for nearly thirty years. My life had been changed by Sharon's illness, losing Haley Rose and the death of several much loved horses. Maybe it was a time for me to think about change too...

CHAPTER FORTY

Free at Last

Getting so disastrously caught in the fence was the final straw. Before this culminating spectacle, Praise Hallelujah had been routinely breaking his fence boards or kicking them loose. One day Marcie, the gal who cleaned the stalls, told me Hallelujah had some boards down. Man, had he! His pen looked like toothpicks scattered around. Most of them were along the fence where the boarded geldings were pastured. He had not torn the complete fence down, so he was still contained, but it would need some major repairs.

Our fences were not puny. The posts were 6 inches in diameter and 8 feet long, pounded in the ground 3 feet with the remaining 5 feet above for boards or mesh fencing. The boards, where we used them, were 2 inch by 6 inch treated lumber. As time went on, his pen was repaired by putting double boards on with a spacer board in between making it doubly strong. Still he broke them in places. Once he even broke the double boards, which I would have thought impossible. If he had been a draft horse, such as a Belgium, weighing a ton, I could have understood it. His method was to run at the fence to get the horses on the other side, hitting the boards with his chest, or he would back up to it and kick them.

I moved him to a small pen on the back side of the barn where he could see the cows and only see the horses from quite a distance. The situation was going from bad to worse. This was no way to keep my prized show horse stallion and my former buddy. I needed to seriously rethink my goals. Hallelujah's last two breeding seasons had been rather odd. His services were not in as much demand, but we still got a few mares.

Pleasure horse people seem to enjoy trying different stallions, and many have their own stallions. The number of mares coming to him was not the strange occurrence; rather it was that we got only a small percentage of them in foal. Especially sad for me was not getting a wonderful show mare in foal. The owner would have shown it, and I am sure the baby would have been superb. After three heat cycles, we agreed he should take her to another stallion where she got in foal the first try. The blame could not be placed on the Hallelujah; his sperm checked out well and his interest in the mares was great. It was frustrating to go through all the work and end up without a pregnant mare.

I try to be in tune with the Grand Plan for my life whatever it turns out to be, and it seemed that quite possibly I was not supposed to be breeding mares any more. Perhaps that phase of my work with horses was at an end. It had been a 30-year run with seven different stallions, and I was proud of that. My boys and I had accomplished a lot in those years.

Yet, truthfully, I found that I no longer had a great passion in breeding horses. It was a lot of work as well as stress, and the last breeding season had been especially stressful. A twenty-year-old mare was shipped in to be bred. She had arthritis and was on medication, but she was still quite lame. She'd been here only a week before she got a bad eye infection—which kept reoccurring. She required constant treatment for one thing or another. She was hard to keep fat enough to look healthy. Sometimes a low grade painful condition such as arthritis can keep a horse thin. Fortunately, it was summer and there was plenty of grass which is more palatable than hay, and she had stayed in relative good flesh. We bred her all summer and into the fall and still didn't get her in foal. The vet thought she was not in correct breeding condition and I agreed. Chronic pain can keep a mare barren. Every time I bred her I felt bad. Maybe I was getting too old and jaded. I contacted the owner several times, hoping he would say to send her home, but he did not. He really wanted a Praise Hallelujah foal.

I had another problem with bringing more horses into this world. Throughout Hallelujah's breeding career, I bought some of his offspring if I heard of their being in poor condition or needing a good home. I couldn't keep on doing this forever. His colts and fillies were more to me than just a breeding fee and possible fame if the young horse turned out to be a great show horse. I felt a responsibility to them. How many more did I want to be accountable for? I had rescued Cookie from an abusive trainer who used the soring method of training. If I bred a great quality horse that was destined to be a show horse, what kind of training methods would he endure? Would I ever know?

The next issue to be considered, strangely enough, was the legislative bill presently, in 2006, before Congress about horse slaughter. HR 503 would make it against the law to kill horses for food here in the United States. We don't eat horse meat, but it's exported to Europe and Japan where it is enjoyed. I would never contemplate sending one of mine to auction for such an end, but about 90,000 horses a year do end up with that fate. How could I be sure one of Hallelujah's offspring wouldn't be one of them? Two of the horses I had rescued which were sired by him had been headed to the killer pen at an auction because of their bad actions due to poor training techniques or ignorance.

HR 503 closed the slaughter plants in the *U.S.*, but didn't stop the transportation of the same poor horses to Mexico or Canada where our USDA had no control over the method of slaughter. *The Farmer's Exchange* December 5, 2008 issue stated "More horses sent abroad after slaughter ban. Killer buyers still show up at auctions to purchase the horses no one else buys, sometimes outbidding a regular buyer. The killer buyers acknowledge that the long trips abroad are stressful on the animals, but they blame animal rights activists who successfully pushed for all U.S horse slaughterhouses to be shut down. They say the increased exportation of horses is better than the alternative: horses being neglected and abused by owners who don't want them or can't afford to take care of them. Slaughter opponents got a hopeful sign from Congress when a proposed export-for-slaughter ban was approved by the House Judiciary Committee in late September '08. The bill got hung up in the Agriculture Committee during the final days of the session and will have to be reintroduced next year."

The other side of the situation was the question: if there was no place to send unwanted horses, what *would* happen to them? Would they be left to starve or die a miserable death of old age? Would there be plentiful horse rescue sites? I didn't know the answers, but I had the overwhelming feeling that I could not be responsible for that happening to any horse I bred, and that meant not breeding any more. I owned six of my own and could plan on long retirements for them and an easy end of life when it became necessary.

In February of 2006, Hallelujah was eighteen and I was sixty-six. For the two previous years I had contemplated gelding him, not because he was hard to handle or didn't produce great colts, but because of his increasing unhappiness and my not being able to enjoy riding him any longer. These issues along with my epiphany that I wasn't to bring any more horses into this world, led me to phone my Amish feed man one morning and ask him an important question. In the *Farmer's Almanac* are dates each month for doing things such as planting, harvesting, weaning and castrating. These dates are dictated by the phase of the moon and its position in the zodiac. Long ago I discovered the advantage of gelding my horses in the proper moon sign. There was little bleeding and less swelling; the horses recovered faster and suffered less discomfort. The Amish are great believers in doing things by the moon, and I knew he would have the right dates.

I wanted to use Dr. Brandt because I liked his method of putting the horse on his back for the surgery. He was too far away to be used for every little veterinarian problem or when a vet was needed extremely quickly, as his practice could take him hours away; but for this important surgery for my special horse, I needed Dr. Brandt. I called two weeks before the date I desired, in order to give Dr. Brandt time to schedule. It is best to do the surgery outside where there would be less contaminates, but what would the weather be like on February 28? We could have a snow storm, it could be rainy with the wind howling, or it could be nice. So far, we had enjoyed a mild winter and I was hoping that day would be as beautiful as possible for the end of February. I woke up during the night before the big day, wondering if I was doing the right thing. I convinced myself that I was and went back to sleep.

The day dawned clear, with no wind whatsoever. It was in the 20s in the morning, but by the time Dr. Brandt arrived at 11 a.m., it was really quite balmy. I remarked to him how nice a day it was, and he replied, "I bet Hallelujah was wishing we had a terrible snowstorm."

"No," I answered, envisioning him eventually running and grazing with his mares, "he wants this. It will be a good thing for him, not a punishment." Over the several decades of dealing with my veterinarians, most of them have come to respect my somewhat unconventional thoughts regarding my animals. Whether they agree or not, they have always been very tolerant. As I led my stallion out the barn door, I was grateful for the beautiful day. We were blessed.

With the warm sun shining down on us, Dr. Brandt gave him a tranquilizer which made him a little woozy, but he stayed on his feet. While he was mixing the anesthetic, which would be injected into Hallelujah's jugular vein, I asked him where his helper was. He always had an assistant when he had come in the past who handed him the surgical instruments. "Well," he said, "she had a class and I told her we were working around the moon, and that was more important than her being there, so we would carry on without her." I hoped she understood about the moon!

About this time, Bob stepped out of the house and asked if we needed any more help. The answer being yes, he came to assist. When the anesthetic is administered one never knows for sure how the horse will react. He might crash to the ground. I hoped Hallelujah wouldn't do that. His bones were eighteen years old after all. After the injection, he just sat down on his haunches like a dog would do, and then rolled over onto his side. How nice that was! We rolled Hallelujah onto his back, Bob steadied the front legs and I held the pan with the instruments. In short order the surgery was performed. There had been no bleeding. All was going very well. The horse lay on the ground for about fifteen minutes while the anesthetic wore off. Getting up can be somewhat hazardous also, both for the people and the horse. Sometimes the patient gets up before he is really fully awake, lurching and stumbling about.

Hallelujah opened his eyes, placed his hind legs underneath him and got up as if in slow motion. Nothing to it, he was calm as could be. "What a wonderful horse," Dr. Brandt remarked. I had always thought so but wondered exactly what he meant right now, so I asked. He explained that Hallelujah's way of getting up was unusual and very good. He had not stressed his surgical area, nor had he strained his muscles or joints. He was very pleased. We walked Hallelujah to the barn. He was a little unsteady, but doing great.

It had been a flawless operation and an ideal day for the last of February. Dr. Brandt had commented on how few days there are in a year when the temperature is mild, there is no wind, the sun is shining, and *there are no flies.* I guess only animal people would think of flies! It was a perfect and promising start to the new life Praise Hallelujah, my exceptional friend, and I were about to embark upon. The sun shone warmly on our backs as my horse and I entered the barn. Hallelujah exuded an aura of calmness that had nothing to do with his rapidly disappearing anesthetic. I was at peace too. I knew I had done the right thing.

CHAPTER FORTY-ONE

My Horse is Back

The vet said it would take thirty days for Hallelujah's testosterone hormone level to be under control or mostly gone. I guess he was right because I tried to put the horse out in his old pasture after two weeks of recuperation and Sarah called me on the phone. "Hallelujah is in the fence again!"

Rats and dang, I could not believe it. When I had left that morning, he was just fine. Bob and I again cut him out. He was caught even worse than before and had been there for some time as the ground underneath him was messy. It had started to snow, and there he was, lying with his hind feet strung up in the air, but flat on his side, no twist this time around. It was the same hock on his right leg and it was really stuck. Bob was about to take a portion of the fence down, but I talked him into just cutting it as before. Fortunately that worked again, and my silly ex-stallion staggered to his feet and limped back to the barn.

More Banamine injections for pain, and more liniment and washing seemed to do the trick because the next day he was walking as though nothing had happened. But I'd learned my lesson and left him in the small pen beside the cows.

Finally, it was thirty days post surgery. The sun was shining after many dreary March days and it was the normal high of 50 degrees. I was itching to ride and Hallelujah was easily accessible. I had already ridden him once ten days earlier and he had been excellent. I stayed in the inside arena, not wanting to take any chances as the mares were in a pasture by the outside arena. Today I was going to try riding outside. I lunged him first. He could see the mares but didn't care. He trotted around his circle like a real gentleman. After ten minutes, I saddled and rode him. He was first rate. We did a flat walk, running walk and canter. As we were doing the running walk, the mares decided to have a mare fit and began squealing at each other. Hallelujah cocked an ear in their direction but kept going. I think he thought, "Hummm, does that require my attention?" Going on with his work, he seemed to answer himself that he didn't need to bother. We didn't ride long; he was out of shape having been stalled and penned during his recuperation. As I brought him back into the barn, I said to Erica, "Believe it or not, this is the way he was when he was a breeding stallion before I quit riding him!" I was happy, and so I think, was Hallelujah.

Hallelujah was fast becoming my favorite horse to ride again, a pleasure I desperately needed. Sharon's health was failing more obviously now. Her true grit was still apparent, but pain was a more constant companion and it showed. I was grateful for any happiness I was given.

On our next ride I got braver. I didn't lunge him first, and he was perfect; so good in fact, that I decided to take him on a short trail ride. The trail went between the mare pasture and the creek, which could have made the ride very interesting! What would he do riding so close to the grazing mares? He flicked his ears and looked towards them but otherwise was fantastic. I didn't go far. I was happy with the short ride. Heading for the barn with Hallelujah in a running walk and me with a big grin on my face, I remembered the past when he was such a delight to ride and show. The next question to be answered would be, "How spooky was he now?" Gelding him wouldn't make him less jumpy than he had been. In fact, some of my stallions after gelding were spookier.

Without the testosterone coursing through their veins and thoughts of mares in their minds, they found other things to occupy their interest. A leaf falling, a squirrel jumping from a tree branch, or things I couldn't even see or hear could make them startle and jump. The cat incident with Hallelujah had been debilitating to me for many weeks and memories of it still lingered. I hoped Hallelujah's surgery wouldn't increase his spookiness. Time would tell. But for now on a warm and freshly green spring day, I sat tall and proud on my best horse and dreamed about a splendid future.

CHAPTER FORTY-TWO

Green Pastures

Hallelujah settled in nicely in his new position as Boss Man without a stallion's driving energy. He still nickered and touched the mares as they passed his stall on their way out to the pasture. If one was in season, we all knew it by his loud squeals as they pranced by; but as soon as they had left, he happily went back to eating or gazing after them. He had his original stallion pasture with some grass, but he kept it pretty well eaten. He had stopped kicking through the fences. He kept his eyes on the mares at times but now it was different–more like watching the girls go by. He was content.

I rode him on the trails occasionally and he got plenty of apples or carrots. I had a sense that he was ready to turn out with the mares, but I had a big trip coming up, so I planned to do it as soon as I got home. I asked Erica to be there early in the morning for the big event which I fervently hoped would be uneventful.

I had the video camera ready and Erica had the camera. We put the mares out first and then let him go. Stallions are great poop sniffers. They can tell a lot about the animal who left the pile. Hallelujah had perfected the routine. If he didn't get a good enough whiff, he would paw at the pile to make it smell fresher. I was pretty sure one of the things he would enjoy doing would be checking out all the piles of horse manure in the pasture.

The mares ran out into the small field I had picked for the occasion, leaving Hallelujah at the barn door where he began checking out the horse droppings. Not much time passed before he trotted into the pasture. The top mare came to meet him giving him a squeal and kicking out at him. He returned the squeal and then it was on to more horse piles. The rest of the mares were grazing hungrily; they had no time for him. After checking the perimeter of the pasture, he dropped his head to eat.

"Well, I'm impressed," Erica said.

Me too!

We left them and I planned on checking frequently to be sure all was still peaceful. A little later in the morning, the boarder who owned the dominant boss mare, came to ride her. Getting her out of the pasture stirred up the herd and there was more squealing and running about. It was hotter than usual that day and Hallelujah looked a little frazzled. He was used to his paddock that attached to his stall where he could go in and out as he pleased, letting the shade cool him. I decided to put him back in the barn. He'd had enough excitement for the first day.

The second day was more of the same except now the mares knew who was in their midst and kept coming up to him to greet and perhaps pay homage. Several were mares he had bred and some were his daughters. They all knew exactly who *he* was. They chewed on his neck with much delight. The problem was, he was being mobbed. The mares were all vying for his attention, and it was getting dicey. I wondered if I would need to step in, but they soon went their way to enjoy the grass. The mares repeated those actions on and off during the day, but they were of short duration. Hallelujah remained with the girls for the complete turnout period. He was the first one wanting to come in for night feeding, standing at the gate into the barn with his head hanging over the boards, but he had survived the sun as well as the ladies' attentions.

The next day I opened the gate to the big 5 acre pasture. Hallelujah had graduated. He had proven himself. This would be real freedom. The early morning grass glistened with dew and a soft, cool breeze rustled Hallelujah's tail and mane ever so slightly. It would soon heat up and be a scorcher again, but for now it was perfect. A light mist hung over the pasture; the mares knew where to go, but it was new to Hallelujah. They all ran off leaving him behind. Suddenly, he threw up his head and galloped at top speed after them disappearing into the misty dawn. Tears glistened in my eyes, but I had a big smile upon my face. My favorite horse was truly free at last.

CHAPTER FORTY-THREE

Sharon's Legacy

Breast cancer activist loses 7-year battle read the headline in one of our December 2004 local newspapers. It was hard for me to see Sharon as an activist, but she was indeed. Over and over she told friends and family, "Breast cancer saved my life." Before breast cancer she had been a highly competitive and extremely talented well-paid regional-development-market manager for Merck.

After her diagnosis, she chose to concentrate her considerable talents and drive toward helping other women with breast cancer. To this end, she focused on the Y-ME National Breast Cancer Organization. She served on committees and, more importantly, helped staff its hotline. She especially wanted to help other inflammatory breast cancer patients. I remember her telling me one day how draining these conversations with other women were. Now and then she felt too bad to take the call, but usually she put on a brave face and did her best. She became a founding member of Y-ME's Illinois affiliate, an organization she held dear to her heart.

Her desire to help others was so strong that she flew many miles to seminars around the country to share her insights. I remember a late night call from San Francisco. The next day she was to make her presentation and her "syndrome" as she called it—severe flu-like symptoms—threatened to incapacitate her. We talked, we cried a bit and then she took more pain medication. By the next morning she had rallied enough to continue.

Three problems facing cancer patients especially concerned her. The first was how to deal with intimacy after a breast cancer diagnosis. She had divorced her husband because she found him part of the problem in her recovery. This was not uncommon, she discovered. Many husbands had a hard time coping with a changed wife.

Another issue she grappled with was the loneliness and isolation a diagnosis of cancer brings. She wept as she told me how her old friends with very few exceptions seldom called or visited. "What do they say?" she asked. "They don't know how to deal with a sick person—one who may die." This led her to strongly believe in peer support and the need to educate others. Her new cluster of friends became other survivors and fighters, a very close-knit group that had little in common with other friends and even family. They were her other family.

The third issue was how cold doctors can be when explaining a cancer diagnosis and treating patients. Sharon put on a whole seminar that was taped for future use by Northwestern University's medical instructors to educate medical students and hospice team members. After her live seminar a young doctor came up to her and said, "Sharon, I had no idea. Thank you very much for opening my eyes."

Though people expected to help, from spouses to health professionals, often fail to handle cancer patients' needs adequately, sometimes complete strangers surprise us. John came into Sharon's life as a blind date. Sharon loved John from the beginning, confiding to me she wondered what he would think of her poor damaged body. But John loved her as a whole person, never seeming to notice the physical ravages of this disease except as it caused Sharon pain. More importantly, he refused to let the future haunt their lives. John said he knew he would eventually lose her, but the two of them centered their lives on the present. Where other couples planned a year, they focused on next week or next month. They refused to worry about the time they wouldn't have. John shared Sharon's reaction, "We're not going to give in to this. How do we adapt?"

Adapting was what she did when she walked down the aisle on Hal's arm at her small and private wedding to "Her John." Barely recovered from spine surgery weeks before to alleviate pressure on her spinal cord and patched together with two steel rods, she did as she had planned. No wheelchair or walker for her. Bravely hiding pain from her well-wishers, she said her vows.

A few days before Christmas, Sharon bid us her final farewell. With all my heart I hope she had a steed as spirited and remarkable as she was herself, to gallop through the gates of Heaven. Perhaps Sir with his Arabian

John and Sharon in Alaska

beauty and big black eyes, grey coat with black mane and tail—the horse with the mischievous sense of humor and the fast gallop. Or maybe Delight, that roguish, handsome, chestnut Tennessee Walking Horse stallion who shared her unique zest for excitement.

One winter evening shortly after she had passed, I was reading *Sometimes a Woman Needs a Horse* by Betsy Kelleher. As I snuggled deeper into my cozy chair, I heard a voice speak inside my mind that was unmistakably Sharon's. "Mom," she said. "*you* should write a book!"

I put my book down and felt a rush of love. Sharon had been gone two months, and I still didn't believe it. Our Sharon was born with a great love for animals, same as me.

One day, several years into her illness, we discussed how different our lives were. In her thirties she had been a high-salaried district manager for Bristol-Meyers Squibb Co., and later a regional-development-market manager for Merck, both top-name pharmaceutical drug companies. I married right out of high school, and my life had been one of having four children plus helping a husband in his chiropractic business. Later, after moving to our small family farm, I added milking cows, gardening, canning vegetables and breeding horses to my agenda. All these things kept me busy, but if I had to go out into the world and get a job, I felt I would be lacking. I lamented those thoughts to Sharon.

"You know, Mom, I should write your life's résumé. If you went through all the things you have done I bet you would be surprised and pleased. You don't have to have a college degree to be successful. You don't have to make a lot of money to be proud. Give me a list, and I will write it for you."

Sharon was good at writing business resumes, having done several for her siblings. I really wanted to do it, but time just got away from me and Sharon became sicker and sicker. She passed away without our producing my life's résumé. Now hearing her speak to me on that quiet evening, I knew she was telling me to write about my life. But where to start? Then it came to me: center the story about the horses she and I both loved. Thus was born the idea for *The Horse That Wouldn't Trot.*

CHAPTER FORTY-FOUR

The Beat Goes On

One-two-three-four; lub-dub, lub-dub, lub-dub—whether the rhythm of the Walking Horse gait or the beating of the human heart—life went on.

I gazed from the kitchen window and saw a very happy and content ex-stallion. Praise Hallelujah, now twenty-one-years old, was becoming pleasingly plump from all that succulent grass. After wearing horse blankets all his life, he now detested them. Subsequent to causing mass destruction to several, I gave up and allowed him his choice. I saw him grazing quietly with Sunday, Nugget, and Black Cashmier—his special mares. Nugget was the old dowager and remained one of my most dependable and enjoyable horses to ride. Cashmier was Hallelujah's special favorite, and Sunday—what can I say about Sunday? She was still ornery, but at eleven, she had mellowed some around the edges. She was still a talented show horse but nowadays our barefoot performances were for our eyes only on the beautiful woodland and green field trails. She was ready to go to a competition any time and blow the other horses out of the water with her elegance and ability. All the other horses had accepted our retirement from the show ring, but according to Mary Long, Sunday still wanted to compete.

These horses had made me. During our show years I was well-known because of them. They deserved and would get care for the rest of their lives.

"Grammy, Grammy! Look what I am wearing!" It was five year-old Alexis Danielle rushing in the door with new cowboy boots on her feet and riding helmet in hand. Three-year-old Ava Marie, not to be outdone, was jumping up and down showing off her blue horsey shirt.

"I want to ride *my* Black Cashmier."

"Me too," Ava chimed in.

Momma horse, Cashmier, now had another job. She was the gentlest, most patient and smallest of the mares. She made the perfect first horse. Alexis had laid claim to her.

"Someday I will ride Nugget (the biggest of my horses) outside all by myself," Alexis said importantly, full of self confidence and sounding for all the world like her Aunt Sharon.

"Me too," Ava insisted.

"Of course you will," I answered, thinking of their Aunt Sharon, Aunt Michal, Mommy Chessa as well as my niece Gabriella, Erica, Shelby and Sara, all the young girls before them who had enjoyed the wind in their hair with blissful smiles on their faces while riding their favorite horses.

Erica wanted to get married on the farm, her "most favorite place in the whole world." It was a stunning affair. She made plans for her horse, Kit, to be included. Sitting in the front row with Erica and Michael's parents, we all expectantly turned our heads toward the west. When the time came to give the bride away, Erica came galloping across the field full of beautiful August wildflowers, veil flowing, wedding dress flying, white cowboy boots sticking out from under her gown, straight to her dad, who helped her dismount and led her down the meadow aisle on his arm. It was a wonderful and fulfilling close to a Heaven-sent ten years with this hard-working and talented young horsewoman.

Erica and Michael gave Hal and me a thank-you note after the wedding. What she wrote to me I shall forever cherish. "Rose, your liveliness and natural gift with horses is something I have admired and attempted to attain. Thanks for teaching me so much. I will miss you dearly…"

And to Hal, "Thanks for supporting your wife and encouraging her to fulfill her dreams. I hope Michael will do the same for me."

In my story only a little is mentioned of Hal, but he cast a big shadow—a shadow of support and understanding of my inner drive to become a horsewoman. He never told me I couldn't or shouldn't do anything. His physical presence was only once at a horse show, but he was the first out of the house to see us upon our return. "How did you do?" he'd ask, and beam at the pile of ribbons and trophies. He could always be counted on to fix the numerous fence breaks, make new fences, mow pasture fields and clean the barn when my barn cleaner was absent. I told friends that fortunately for me, Hal loved working on the farm instead of playing golf. I could never have reached my goals without him. (Love ya, honey.)

Alexis, Hal, Rose and Ava
Photo by Rachel Scroggins

With Erica leaving the area and beginning married life, my show career finally came to a close. Without someone young to do most of the physical work, share the fun and encourage me to keep competing, the end of that aspect of my life had arrived. However, Bob had an idea: he took me to the Grand Canyon to ride the mules down to the bottom and then back up the next day. "We need to go before you get any older," he said not so jokingly.

I fell in love with Charley, my Grand Canyon mule. It was true that all through my life when God closed one door, He opened another. I was about to walk through this new door and embark upon another great life adventure with mules. But that is another story...

AFTERWORD:

The Crusade Continues

The question remains: are Tennessee Walking Horses better off in 2009 than in 1970? The short answer is yes, in that the outright abuse was stopped. No more blood and open wounds are allowed, but the secret, hidden, uncaring cruelty has continued in too many cases.

On February 8, 2006, the USDA hosted a listening session with Walking Horse enthusiasts, trainers, owners and breeders about the Horse Protection Act and its enforcement. Dr. Behre, then Horse Protection coordinator for Animal Care at the USDA, discussed soring and incidences of soring that he had seen or heard about at shows over the past few years. He explained that he wandered about the show grounds as a spectator might and discovered some truths about soring first hand. He discussed the scar rule which was a hotly debated issue between trainers and inspectors. (Many trainers insisted scars were normal, not caused by their training techniques.)

He showed slides of other horses in different disciplines that are subjected to mud, sweat and friction. These horses showed no scars or tissue changes. Slides of American Saddlebreds and Hackney Ponies that also use action devices such as chains, commonly on all four limbs, also showed no tissue changes or scars. He discussed Tennessee Walking Horses that are ridden for pleasure or are backyard pets, stating they show no tissue changes, so it could not be a "breed characteristic." Also the back pasterns of show animals are free from changes which also were exposed to the same mud, sweat and motion. In his opinion, the cause of scaring must be the application of chemicals. The scar rule would remain a hot topic for years to come.

I didn't show my horses during the 2006 season, so I was somewhat out of touch with the industry. When it was time for the 2006 TWHBEA Celebration, I got some interesting emails from friends. On August 25, trainers angered by the strict USDA inspection process refused to bring their horses to be checked, resulting in a standoff, the summoning of police and the postponement of several events. One of Praise Hallelujah's great show daughters was being exhibited and the mare's owner kept me apprised.

The 2006 TWH National Celebration ended in an uproar without crowning a World Grand Champion for the first time ever, when the USDA inspectors disqualified six of the ten finalists and because of conflict, the class was cancelled. For a show season that had started out on a positive note, things sure fell apart at the biggest show of the year.

2008 didn't prove to be much better according to a July 2008 *Lexington Herald-Leader* article which stated that "One of the largest walking horse shows in Kentucky virtually ground to a halt last week when U.S. Department of Agriculture inspectors arrived, escorted by Kentucky State Police." And Keith Dane, director of equine protection for the Humane Society of the United States (HSUS), said that it had not been uncommon this year for competitors to leave rather than face prosecution. I was certainly disappointed with the continuing and blatant disregard for the Horse Protection Act.

In August 2008, The American Association of Equine Practitioners (AAEP) recommended "altering judging standards to no longer reward the 'manufactured' exaggerated gait of the Tennessee Walking Horses." The AAEP called soring "one of the most significant welfare issues affecting any equine breed or discipline today."

I talked at some length with a well-known sound pleasure horse trainer who competes favorably even with sored pleasure horses at the highest level who has observed some of the padded big lick show horses in their show stalls, playing and jumping about. In this trainer's opinion, it is the *pleasure* show horse that is the most at risk. As stated earlier in the story, the pleasure horses are sored in more undetectable ways (pressure shoeing, etc) and suffer continuously.

This trainer says some trainers want to show sound or at least sounder show horses, but they have a big problem and guess what it is?—the owners. If a trainer of a big lick or pleasure show horse doesn't put a winning horse in the ring, the owner moves the horse to a trainer who will use any method that gets the blue ribbons.

We talked about the spectators and how they either are the problem or contribute to it. When show horses enter the ring "crawling and crankin" (sored horses whose hind hocks nearly touch the ground and the front legs wave the air) the audience cheers loudly. The cheering of spectators was what actually set the stage for the trainers of the big lick Tennessee Walking Horses upon their disgraceful journey.

In pre-World War II days, the Walkers at the shows were utility animals and were to be judged as such. But the crowd didn't care for them, preferring the cocky Saddlebred. The trainers tried to make the Walkers more sprightly and exciting, succeeding to a point; but instead of continuing on that path, they started down the wrong road of chemically soring to make a spectacular show horse—one the crowds loved.

Another problem is the judging. What the judges place and give blue ribbons to, is what's desired. It is said the judges could put a stop to this madness now, except they are themselves trainers and no one wants to take the first step. I had the same problem showing Hallelujah. A few judges rewarded the natural horse; most did not.

My mom had a saying, "Don't throw the baby out with the bath water," meaning don't throw the good out with the bad. Show horses comprise only about 3 percent of the total registered Tennessee Walking Horses, but they get the publicity. In despising the soring and other inhumane treatment of this percentage, the public should also be aware of the greatness of the breed and the new vision of some in the industry's organizations. The FEI World Equestrian Games which are to be held in 2010 in Lexington, Kentucky, are allowing the versatile and sound Tennessee Walking Horses to participate. They will perform in jumping, reining, driving and bitless demonstrations. (There will be no padded performance big lick horses permitted.) Showcasing the breed as versatile and pleasurable will go a long way in showing the public the other side of the Tennessee Walking Horse story. We can discourage soring by rewarding the sound Walking Horse.

To hear the very latest on the soring issue and what was to be done about it in 2009, I attended the Second Annual Sound Horse Conference, put on by FOSH (Friends of Sound Horses). One of the presentations on video was of trainers who had used the soring method and now wanted to expose it. Because of fear of retribution, their stories were read by an anonymous person. Told in detail, their accounts left me sickened.

Rachael Cezar, D.V.M. told us the 2009 show season would be different. The scar rule would be *strictly* enforced; saddles would not be allowed on horses during inspections because irritating objects had been discovered under the girths of some horses which irritated the animals so they would ignore pain caused by palpation inspections.

For me, the most exciting new happening, was the increased use of improved thermography for inspections. As explained and shown by slides, thermography picks up heat emitted in the form of infrared radiation. The skin is almost perfect for emitting heat patterns which show increased blood flow and inflammation. Sore tendons, hot spots in the foot and around the ankles showed red; and dark areas were seen where a masking or numbing agent had been applied. No hidden abuses would sneak by. Feet would be inspected for illegal shoeing. Shoes might be pulled and inspected.

Keith Dane of the Humane Society of the United States suggested everyone write their congressmen and urge more funding for the USDA to do their job. The annual $500,000.00 that was originally allocated in 1970, has never been increased (or adjusted to allow for inflation) and allows only a small number of shows to be attended by the USDA.

Public opinion holds great sway. The movement to expose and clean up the Walking Horse show industry got a monumental boost in 2006, with the articles on soring that were written in *Equus, The Horse, Horse Illustrated* and other publications. Before this, soring was a fairly well kept secret from the many horse lovers and owners outside the Walking Horse breed.

I waited to close this chapter on the crusade to end soring until after the 2009 Walking Horse Celebration. Change seems to be in the wind, but it does not diminish the reality that some show horses are still being sored. Dr. Cezar was quoted in the August 23, 2009, *The Tennessean* newspaper, just days before the start of the 2009 Celebration, "It is not as blatant as it was 40 years ago, but it still exists and we are working on ways to detect it even when it is more subtle."

The USDA inspectors *were* tough on the Celebration inspections and caught a lot of violations. The scar rule was strongly enforced. This is very important as future training methods will not be allowed to create scars and horses with scars will be retired from showing. Because of the tough inspections, the Celebration classes were small. One of the pleasure championship classes only had one exhibitor! The big lick classes were also small and the general consensus of people I spoke to was that the horses that got into the ring were "sounder" but not sound. Some horses were given violation tickets on the way *out* of the ring after being observed in their classes.

A remark made by a young Walking Horse trainer to my friend Lori at one of the big 2009 spring shows where the USDA had shown up in force and few horses were being shown because of it, hopefully portends better things to come.

He lamented to her, "I wish I'd listened to my daddy and gone to college instead."

The Tennessee Walking Horse is an amazing breed. I agree with a comment made to me by Dr. Dave Whitaker that if the Walking Horse industry had patterned themselves after the Quarter Horse instead of the showy Saddlebred horses, the Tennessee Walking Horse could have been the breed second in popularity after the Quarter Horse. They are a multi-faceted, intelligent horse with smooth gaits, gentle, loving dispositions and with proper training can excel on many different levels.

Remember: Ride one today, and *you* just might buy one tomorrow. I did!

New Book Preview

Longears and Broomtails:
A Mule Story about the Adventures and Misadventures of a New
Mule Owner

Chapter One
My Grand Canyon Mule Charlie

When Bob, who was the same age as our oldest daughter, Sharon, and became like an adopted son to my husband and me, suggested that I go with him to the Grand Canyon and take the mule ride to the bottom and back to the top while I was still young enough to do it, I dismissed the idea. I thought perhaps I was already too old. I had two cranky knees and an even crankier back. The knees were brought on by horse events, one of them quite serious, and my back was the reason I rode Tennessee Walkers, a smooth *gaited* horse, on *flat* surfaces.

Bob had hiked the Canyon three times and had done the day ride on the mules once. The day ride was a journey to the lunch point at Indian Gardens and then back up on the same Bright Angel Trail the same day. Bob didn't ride the horses we owned preferring to walk the dogs around the same farm trails that I reveled in enjoying from horseback. The fact he was willing to ride a mule four hours down and five hours back up the Grand Canyon was astonishing to me. Bob has a special love and affinity for the great Canyon and wanted to share it with me even if it meant riding a mule for a large part of two days.

I filed the idea in the back of my mind not giving it serious consideration. I was one year into recovery from my badly twisted knee and was finally riding my own horses again, but the thought of riding hours and miles downhill and back up made me shudder.

"We should make reservations," Bob said, "they need to be made a year in advance because they are limited and very popular. If you can't go, we can cancel."

Well, that made it a possibility at any rate, so I said "yes." We decided on the two day ride going down to the bottom and staying at Phantom Ranch for dinner and the night, and then riding back up and out the next day.

During the succeeding year, my knees made great progress, my back stayed together and nothing else happened to make me hobble. The trip was on! It seemed like it would never get here, but suddenly, it was just a month away. I researched all I could find on the internet about the rides, reading several experiences of other riders. It appeared I could do it if only my knees wouldn't become my "Achilles heel." It is very stressful on knees going downhill as we would be doing.

Late evening on May 11, 2006, we arrived at the El Tovar hotel on the south rim of the Grand Canyon. Between air and car travel we had been on the go for 13 hours and I almost literally fell asleep eating my supper. The next morning we were to be at the mule corral by 6:45. We arrived at the appointed time, but where were the mules? There were strict regulations as to clothing, health requirements and your fear factor. The temperature was hotter than usual. It would be 90 to 100 degrees as we got lower. Bob had chosen the middle of May because the wildflowers and cactus should be in bloom and it *should* be moderate temperatures. Well, one out of two wasn't bad.

After waiting for half an hour, Bob pointed out the mules coming across the road from their barn and pens. There were several wranglers each leading a "bunch" of mules. The mules were tied to each other with about a two and a half foot piece of rope between them. We decided they had the people get there early and have *them* wait on the mules rather than the other way around. The mules had the right of way whether on the trails in the Canyon with hikers—or the buses on the road. As the mules came across, traffic stopped and waited—and waited. It takes awhile for thirty mules or so to slowly cross a road.

I wondered how they would all fit in the small corral, but the wranglers packed them in with only inches between them. Some mules had a few disagreeable looks for their neighbor, but for the most part they stood ears flopped off the sides with a sleepy look in their eyes, resting on a cocked hind leg. They'd been there before and seen it all. The wranglers poked and pushed mule butts over and squeezed in to tie them up with their rope halters. Each mule had his bridle hanging on the saddle horn, which was soon put on his head.

Next, Marilyn, the mule boss, started her speech about the rules of the trail. Everybody hung around the rail and listened raptly to every word she spoke. We were admonished to drink plenty of water out of the little canteens we had been given the night before. Dehydration was a possibility with the weather in the 90s. We were told the mules had the right of way; the hikers had to stand by the side and let us pass. Bob would have good reason to remember that admonition.

The most important rule was that the mules were to be kept head to tail, there were to be no big gaps between them. "A tight compact group was 95 percent of the safety of the trip. If your mule lags behind, it will miss its buddies and then could run to catch up. The ones behind that one would run also." Having greenhorn riders on running mules could be a disaster. Later I wondered why the mule would lag behind if it missed its buddies, but what did I know? We were given a small whip to *beat* our mule's rear end if it fell behind even a little bit. We were impressed that no little gentle taps would do the trick. We had to *mean* it. That should pose no problem for me; after all, I was an experienced horseperson.

I will remember *that* rule to my dying day.

I had already decided to not utter a word about all my horse experience. I had ridden, trained and shown horses for thirty years. I had bred mares, standing at stud seven stallions at one time or another, foaled mares and broke young horses. At different times on our farm I had up to fifty horses for which I was responsible. Nope, I wasn't saying a word. I thought if I did, they might give me a mule that needed some extra ability and I was on vacation. I didn't want any kind of a challenge...

LaVergne, TN USA
04 January 2010

168871LV00001B/29/P